# WHERE DO YOU GO
# WHEN THE PARTY IS OVER

# WHERE DO YOU GO
# WHEN THE PARTY IS OVER

## A.J. MENDEZ

authorHOUSE®

*AuthorHouse™*
*1663 Liberty Drive*
*Bloomington, IN 47403*
*www.authorhouse.com*
*Phone: 1-800-839-8640*

*Published by AuthorHouse    11/26/2012*

*ISBN: 978-1-4772-8672-2 (sc)*
*ISBN: 978-1-4772-8671-5 (e)*

*Library of Congress Control Number: 2012920707*

# THE PREFACE
Written By: A.J. MENDEZ

This book was written to share the most inner feelings of one person during what turned out to be an eye, mind and heart opening experience? Let me give you some insight to this person. This person was given enough warnings concerning the consumption and abuse of alcohol. The damages not only from the medical stand point, but also family traits that have been established within our family tree (that's right I am this person). The consumption of alcohol has indeed taken its toll on my family. Unfortunately, I paid no attention to these warnings.

So it is through this story I will try to explain my existence and how I choose to live my life. For the most part I thought I had lived life to its fullest.

Most certainly this story will not try and cover my entire life, but rather a small portion of my early years and the last five years of my life with my drinking problem, illness and then the search for the truth. For years I thought everything I did and said was done with a good heart and truth, and then I came to realize this bit of honesty. In what seemed like a dream, this portion of the story began to play in my head . . . . started out with me walking up to the edge of a cliff. I had come to a complete stand still and couldn't help but notice the vast sea of damage that was done to the innocent people with whom I had come in contact with and how I was responsible for causing pain and hurt to all of them. What I considered then, was my logical method of handling my personal life now seems to escape any intelligent explanation.

I couldn't help but to ask myself if there was one last miracle left in this aging and tiring body of mine. A better question for those of us, who believe in GOD, would have been, did HE have one final blessing for me?

Would He consider me worth anymore of His time and effort? Could and would He send from the heavens above the help I now would need to continue my life? The thought that came next, was GOD had answered my question with a question of His own. Was this the same man that had ignored all the signs and clues He had already sent to me? Now where would I look to? I needed to find a simpler appropriate start to my story?

How was it that I had caused this much damage to myself and others? How was this possible for me to wind up walking through life not only as a lost soul but living my life in total denial.

What would become of me in trying to live up to my expectations as well as those of other important people in my life? After all I had a lot to live up to as far as trying to prove to my friends and family. Once I was on top of the world and I was invincible.

Before we start the story of my last five years, let's begin when I was seventeen years of age, when I was a shy and inexperienced young man when it came to dealing with women. I was visiting a town not that far from my home town on a Friday night. I was introduced to a sixteen year old very pretty young Hispanic girl (or at least I thought she was Hispanic, I'll explain later).

She was not only a warm and friendly teen, but she seemed to actually like me. We talked for what seemed to be a few moments, but in reality were actually several hours. We became friends and started to meet at more parties and events. I finally got up enough nerve to ask her to dance with me and she accepted. The song was slow and required me to hold her close to my body. She was a quite smaller woman, height wise. I told her to step up on my feet and hopefully she would not feel I was too tall for her. She just smiled and got on top of my feet. The dance went well and ended too quickly as far as I was concerned.

The party ended and then she invited me to join her at her parents' home the following week-end and I accepted.

I was very nervous upon my arrival at her residence and I was introduced to her older brother as he was leaving. The first thought that came to my mind, was I should not say or do anything wrong. Her older brother was much bigger than I was and seemed muscular where I knew I had very little bulk. After his departure, for the first time we were alone and I had A great desire to learn more about her. She sensed my nervousness and did all she could to make me relax.

As time went on, I indeed did become more relaxed and the conversation was coming a lot easier for me.

She not only cleared up some confusion I had about her, but she would also inform me of her feelings for me. After spending some time with her I felt it was time to depart, so I stood up and before I realized what was happening, she was standing in front of me. She was not only blocking the only exit out of her mobile home, but she had a look on her face that had me thinking, was she waiting for a kiss? I walked closer to her and I walked up to her and she made it very clear to me, she intended to give me a very warm and sincere kiss. after the very passionate kiss and hug, I exited her home and this would be the last time I would see her for some time. You must understand, I did not think I deserved this pretty young teen. I was not muscular or good looking. Two weeks after leaving her, I got a letter from her. In this letter she expressed her true feelings for me. She explained she was falling in love with me. Whatever the reason,

I did not respond to her letter or go see her again. As it turned out, she would be the first of many people who came in contact with me that I would ultimately hurt.

Not only physically at times but emotionally. I never realized this until sobriety hit me and I became much more honest with myself and others.

Now I began to reflect on the present, on how my life had come to a bewildering stop and wondered how much life was left in my tiring, aging body and mind. How could I be solely responsible for so much damage, to so many people? As I stood there, I wanted so badly to run and hide behind a bottle of vodka.

I had hidden this particular alcohol often and found it to be as secure as my bedroom was I spent a great deal of time when I was growing up. Was there going to be enough time and energy left for me to correct any portion of this smoldering rubbish that was left behind in the wake of my destruction?

How many of these people really wanted to hear from me again? These questions and many more began to race through my mind. My thoughts seemingly turned back the hands of time, so that I could begin to recall the beginning of what turned out to be the scheduled beginning of the ending of my life, May 4th 2007.

I was lying down on my doctor's examination table as his hands were on my stomach and he was informing me that my Liver was enlarged and very tender. He went on to say that I would have to quit drinking alcohol for at least one year and that I was going to have to try to lose some of the 230 lbs. my body was now carrying.

Not only was I drinking too much, but I love and craved dearly, eating the wrong kinds of food. So on the Fifth of May, better known as the Cinco De Mayo, I began my one year sabbatical from alcohol and began implementation of my weight loss program. But what of the people I had emotionally damaged? I certainly did not want to consider any of my options and have to face those innocent people that were now seemingly floating in front of me in that vast sea that seems to surround me. All these people from my past seem to be staring at me as to be waiting for my next move. How was I going to tell them how truly sorry I was?

How was I going to convince them of my sincerity? Surly tears of sorrow streaming down my guilt ridden face would not be enough.

Then reality took hold of my throat as to remind me the end of my life could be upon me even sooner had been predicted. I began to recall the rest of my saga. While I was recounting the initial days of my sobriety, something came over me forcing me to remember all that dared to stand in my way at one time or another. Whether it was for my own good or them we're trying to make a point. So I started to point my finger at all those who were responsible for my current dilemma?

The list was endless and now a smile had returned along with the satisfaction of knowing I was only a small portion of the problem. After all, certainly I was not a cruel and sadistic person. So where to start? The wise say, it is best to start at the beginning of my scheduled demise. I can only hope in the following pages some of you may be able to relate to my particular circumstance as it unfolds before those who have ventured to read this story. If I have learned anything, my story is not unique. I am not the only one who thought the world revolved around them. Even worse than that, at one time I thought the world rotated because I said it could.

# WHO THE HELL DID I THINK I WAS!!!!!!!!

# Chapter 1

I was done working for the day. I was in the mist of working on my second career. It was another nice sunny day in the San Diego area and I had finished both careers, I was employed to do were in the same field, just different employers. I had just begun my five mile walk. My walking track would take me into a rather deep canyon. Even though there was a paved sidewalk through the canyon, wild life could be easily seen. All animals, those who are non-meat eaters and the ones who were hunting them for their next meal.

The aromas and odors from surrounding plant life were somewhat familiar to me. I began, in my mind to replay all that had happened to me. I had spent thirty six years of my life consuming vast quantities of alcohol. Now I was in the mist of enjoying my second career after what turned out to be a life changing doctor's examination. I had also been employed by the Federal Government for twenty six years. I had reached retirement age right after my fiftieth birthday.

Trying to follow my doctors' advice, I was now exercising every day and the consumption of any alcohol products had been removed from my daily routine.

I concluded my last three years of my career with the Federal Government, mostly work that had nothing to do with my career field. I had joined a committee known as the HEPC (Hispanic Employment Program Committee). We would try to improve the percentage of minorities that were employed in our field. I also joined the Hispanic Coalition. We, as an organized group, tried to find methods to offer scholarship money to minorities for higher education. My mother came to visit me in July for my birthday and I had already lost twenty pounds, but aging years had not been kind to me. My physical appearance was something wanted to hide from her.

It was a look on my face, one of embarrassment and of my health issues. She had noticed I had become sickly looking and advised me it was time for this aging old man to come home. Home was a small town in central northern part of California.

So I took her advice and made preparation for moving all of my possessions and myself back to the town I grew in. All was going well up until the middle of September, and I had already lost thirty pounds. At that point I became bed ridden (I can only presume because of the pain, that I had hurt my back, since that was where the pain seemed to initiate from).

I hired a friend to assist me in keeping my home clean and myself fed. I called my doctor and told him what had happened and he advised me to come in to take some X-Rays of my back. I informed him I had already made arrangements to move back to my home town and would seek out a doctor and have the X-Rays completed.

On October 31st, another friend (this friend has remained in my life) and I began the eight hour drive to my intended new home (which in fact was my parents' home) and at first all went according to the plan I had outlaid.

With only one hour left in our drive I tried to reposition my legs because they were becoming rather sore due to having been in one position so long.

My legs would not respond to my request to reposition and I knew I was in more trouble than I had first imagined. I phoned home, and my father answered and I asked him if any of my nephews or any other lads were at his house.

He responded, yes. I advised him to keep them because I was in need of assistance. We arrived at my home and my nephews quickly responded by helping me out of my car and into my bedroom and into my bed that I would be spending the next year lying on. I found a doctor and on Nov. 4th I went to see her for the first time. My mother and I drove into my new doctors parking lot and we noticed there was two EMT's standing next to their emergency truck. I asked them to assist me out the car and I informed them I had a walker and they assisted me in removing it from our auto. My mother and I then walked into my doctor's office and sat on a sofa. We really did not say much to each other, I believe this had to do with the examination we both felt was not going to bring us good news. Finally my turn came and I got on the scale to weigh myself and surprisingly, I was now weighing 165 lbs. I wondered, could this be possible since I had not exercised in the last month and a half. The nurse lead me to the examining room and started to take my vitals.

We share some small talk and were awaiting for the doctors arrival. The doctor walked in and her first question was, what the purpose of my visit. I started to tell her my story and the pain I was in. She asked me if I could stand up one leg? The look on my face gave her the answer. She told me to lie on her table so she could continue her examination of my sickly, thin looking body.

She pushed on my stomach, and I let out a scream that left no doubt I was in a great deal of pain. She checked my eyes and requested I should remain on her examination table. She left the examination room for about fifteen minutes, and when she returned she advised me she had called the EMT'S to take me to the nearest hospital.

To my surprise, the same two EMT's who had assisted me when I first arrived, were the same two who were now putting me on their bed with wheels. I would spend the next five days in this very well kept hospital. On the fifth day my doctor who was in charge of conducting my test came to my room and informed me he had bad news and worse news. Naturally I asked him to start with the bad news and he complied. He informed me the reason I was having trouble walking was I had fourteen stress fractures in my lower back and that two of them were located near the spinal cord.

He informed me I had ruptured my hernia on the right side of my groin and the knot was the size of a golf ball. This would need to be surgically repaired. He also informed me that my gall bladder was shooting stones into my stomach, and this also would require surgery.

This diagnosis would help me understand why I was so sick all of the time. Additionally he found 10 grade 1 varices in my esophagus that would need to be repaired.

I thought if this was the bad news, what the hell was the worst news? He informed me my Liver was no longer functioning normally. The medical term was cirrhosis of the liver caused by my excessive drinking.

Furthermore he explained he was transferring me to a Liver Transplant Hospital, this would be located in the city of San

Francisco. Before I could consider the trip to San Francisco, I would need to get my Varices (pollups) fixed.

This would help my doctor assure the new hospital that particular problem had been dealt with and corrected.

It was at this time that my new doctor and I found out how much we disagreed on our choice of Sport Teams.

Not that this information has anything important to do with the story. It certainly proved rather entertaining as our relationship grew and made for fun conversation.

We would spend much more time together than either of us could have imagined.

So on first week of January I reported to the recommended hospital in San Francisco for a two week stay. During this period they did a variety of test on and administer drugs to me with my current condition. In the mist of taking all these new drugs and going through the tests, this hospital staff came in one day and told me they were moving me to another room. I shared this double occupancy room with an elderly man who was getting over a serious infection. This move resulted in me getting a triple infection in my stomach. It took me only a matter of hours to contract his infection.

In fact it only took a matter of four hours.

I was rushed to the ICU (Intensive Care Unit) wing with a temperature of 102 degrees. In the ICU wing I was surrounded by doctors and nurses whom seemed sincerely concerned about my health. They were using terms and phrases that were new to me and there seemed to be confusion about my diagnosis.

Needles and tubes were stuck into my neck where my major veins were located. I was then administered a drug and fell into a deep sleep. Later when I awoke a male nurse explained to me how serious my illness was.

He further informed me that I was very jaundiced and anemic and my weight was now a whopping 140 lbs.

I spent the next two days in the ICU wing and then I found out no one had called my family or informed them what had occurred.

Needless to say my mother who is part Mexican and part American Indian went on the War Path. Thank God the taking of scalps is now outlawed or my mother would have been wearing quite a collection (remembering my childhood, I recalled that angry look she possessed). I had three days left of my two week stay and I could not wait for the day to come when they would release me to come home. I recall my mother coming to visit me on one of my final days and I started to weep in her arms and explained to her that my feelings were these professional people were trying to end what was left of my life.

Finally the day came for my release and my nurse had come to inform me to put my street clothes on and the doctor would be up to see me in ten to fifteen minutes. My doctor finally arrived and gave me my diagnoses.

He explained that the doctor at the first hospital was correct with the information he had given me. He told me it was time for me to go home and get plenty of rest and to try to eat whatever I could consume and keep down.

He further stated the importance of taking my medications at the appropriate time. My first question to him was the most obvious. When was I supposed to return to have my Gall Bladder removal or hernia repair surgery? All he could do was simply look at me with no smile on his face or any other positive look. He informed me I would not be returning to the hospital, but rather he had given my sister and mother a package of forms that needed to be filled out as quickly and legally as was possible.

So once again I inquired about the need for surgery and he then informed me that I was not strong enough to survive surgery of any sort.

He continued to amplify his explanation with the following information. My red blood cells were dwindling and my body was no longer making any more of them.

All my male hormones and my important vitamins were Completely depleted, furthermore my liver was functioning at about ten percent of normal. This made surgery an option that could not be considered.

Naturally I inquired what options of any were open to me and he informed me there were no longer any options left.

My next question was a clarification in laymen terms. I asked him if he was telling me I was dying.

He answered rather quickly with a nod of his head to inform me indeed I was dying. I asked him how long did I have left in this world. Once again in a rather quick fashion he answered maybe a week, but certainly no longer than one month. To say my mouth dropped open, is putting it mildly. I was dying and there was nothing I could do to prevent it. He informed me how it was most likely going to take place. He said if I was lucky it would happen late at night while I was asleep and there was a good chance I would not feel a thing, but rather simply to sleep—forever.

Never had loneliness felt so engulfing and the simplest act of breathing had become rather difficult.

The fight I had to muster up to stop the flowing of tears was indeed more than I could handle at this time; I did my best to hide them. I was then put into a wheelchair and escorted out of this hospital. On the way out of this I kept thinking, what was I going to do about my situation and what was going to be the best way to handle this piece of news my doctors had just given me? Had all those parties and late night activities been worth the condition my body was suffering? More importantly, what was left for me to do (NOW THAT ALL THOSE PARTIES WERE OVER)?

What was left for me to consider? All I could come up with, I wanted to be laid to rest in my home town. What of these doctors who were supposed to have a solution for my illness?

Doctors who gone to numerous years of school and had gained much knowledge.

# AFTER ALL:

# THESE DOCTORS HAD JUST TOLD ME TO GO HOME AND DIE!!!!!!

# Chapter 2

To say the ride home took forever is indeed an understatement. When we finally arrived at my parents' home I was assisted once again to my bedroom and when I started to take my clothes off and slip into my shorts and one of my many sport jerseys, I notice the nurse had forgotten to take the needles and portions of lines from the IV'S were still attached to my arm. My mother called my local GP doctor and told her what had happened and the doctor told her sternly not to touch the needles, but rather get me into her office as soon as possible. Before I knew what was happening I was on the way to my doctor's office for removal of the needles and attachments. My doctor could not believe they had forgotten to remove the needles and asked what the rest of the service was like.

We recounted all that had happened and she took notes, we were never told what she did with those notes. We returned to our humble abode and I fell asleep rather quickly. When I awoke my sister and I began to fill out the forms the doctor had given her.

The first one of course was my last Will. This particular form took us the rest of the day to fill out, because I wanted to leave something for all my favorite nephews and nieces.

Then it was time to write down what my son would receive and what would be left to my parents. We would finally conclude this Last Will and I was growing quite exhausted.

We decided to start fresh the next morning. To say that sleep came easy for me was nothing compared to the difficulty I experienced when I got sick every time I tried to eat some food. Later when we got to the rest of the forms, they were a lot easier to fill out and complete. It wasn't until we got to the last form trouble once again reared its ugly head. I asked my sister to please send in my youngest sister whom also resided in our small town only a few blocks from my parents' home. My youngest sister walked in and I told her to please grab a seat.

I was holding the form in my hands and my sister knew something difficult was about to land in her lap.

I looked at her and I asked her if she knew what had happened at the hospital and she answered, yes. I then informed her I needed from her while showing her the form with my signature already on it. This was not a request; this was not going to need much explanation. I told her what it came down to was I needed her to end my life. I went on to tell her, if the doctors had pronounced me brain dead, it was going to be her responsibility to have the doctors pull the plug, because there was no way I was going to be kept alive with machines.

She said she could not do what I was asking. I then informed her I was not asking, I was begging.

Both of my brothers live to far away and my oldest sister lived two hours away. I knew my mother or father could not complete the task and my son was still living in Southern California. There was no one left to fulfill my dying request.

After a little more conversation she finally agreed to make her commitment to my request and I thanked her for stepping up and helping her second oldest of three brothers. She then informed me she needed a drink and I told her I wished that I could join her, but under the present set of circumstances this was not possible.

In preparation of my upcoming event, I decided to ask a friend of the family to become my care giver. She came to my parents' home three times a week to massage my back and to dispense my 28 pills into their appropriate boxes, so I would know which pills to take at their appropriate time in my four phases of my day. I also had to wear a patch on my back which would aid in returning my hormones back you my body.

They needed to be changed daily and I was supposed to drink this thick syrup four times a day.

This syrup would make me spend a great deal of my time traveling between my bedroom and my restroom. Needless to say, taking the pills was not too difficult, but the God awful syrup was enough for me to start to welcome the thought of dying (I did not know how close I was to fulfilling this particular desire). I was **not** 100% committed to watching my food intake and the drinking of that syrup was becoming very difficult and a medicine I no longer wished to consume. (The lack of this syrup would have disastrous results in my stomach). A week past and I received a piece of mail from the San Francisco Hospital.

It was a bill for all the service, test and Doctors opinions along with their diagnosis while I was at their hospital. This document itemized all of the services and medications given to me. The total came to $155,000.00.

A small price to pay for those doctors to conclude that I should go home and die. As I was scanning the four pages of charges, I noticed there was a letter attached to the final page.

The final page simply stated why I was rejected for a liver transplant. They went on to write that they had some ideas and opinions that could help change their original decision.

The first suggestion was, I needed to attend AA meetings. The first question that popped into my mind, was Alcohol Anonymous really going to teach me how to die?

My next question was going to be very simple. All I needed to do was, were these people going to show me how to close my eyes? I thought this part would be reality easy.

They went on to say they would be happy to review my progress in six months or so. The next thought that came to my mind was what were there their real intentions?

Were these doctors going to come and dig up my remains to see if I now qualified for the transplant?

Needless to say whether I agreed with the doctors proposals of attending AA meetings or not and believe me I had no intentions of attending. My thoughts I was having played no part of my family thoughts. The following Tuesday came and my younger sister and mother walked into my room a couple of minutes before 7:00pm to inform me there was an "AA" meeting that night and it was time for me to get out of bed and get dressed and ready myself to go. The child part in me took over and I threw a fit, declaring I was not going to have anything to do with this event. My sister and mother sat me up, knowing full well I could not defend myself.

They cleaned me up and dressed me and I knew I was not going to have a say in the outcome. I needed my walker to assist in entering the AA Room, I sat down on the chair most closely to the exit and sat there staring at people daring them to try and talk to me. The meeting started and ended without me saying one word . . . I took my form up to the person who seemed to be in charge. He signed and dated my form and we went back home. This procedure would happen again with the same result. I do remember there was a time I was at these meetings and they were lasting an hour to an hour and a half.

It was during these times, I would get sick and have to somewhat interrupt the proceedings to get myself to the nearest bathroom. Needless to say when I was finished and returned to my chair, it felt like hundreds of eyes were following me. I thought what do I care what these people think of me, since I wanted nothing from them.

I was not ready to learn or to even understand these people who have similar stories as mine. I was feeling so sorry for myself and I wanted no one to interrupt my solitude. I was going to die and there was nothing they could do about it. My anger would continue every time I attended one of these meetings.

I would later be advised that I was not anyone special.

After all these people in this AA room had seen so many men and women come and go and many them had the same look on their face that I was carrying around with me.

# Chapter 3

The following chapter is for those of you, who like me had no true understanding of the AA process and the message it can carry to those who have lost the ability to drink sociably rather than, as a solution to reality and the problems that may come along the way to distract us.

To say I fully understand the AA process would be a false indication. This is merely to give you as a reader of this book a better understanding of what the AA process has meant to me and how I have adopted in my everyday life.

Meetings for this home group were conducted by—weekly in our small town.

The meetings were conducted by a secretary, who is responsible for opening the meeting by reading the prescribed pages set by the Board Members. Getting a person to chair the meeting (telling the group their personal story). This person would spend 5-15 minutes enlightening the group as to their story about their drinking problem, what they were like then and now AA had made their life better. They also had the option of reading some material from one of the designated AA books.

Then the meeting is opened up to those who wish to share similar stories of their own. The group also needed volunteers to do other service work during, before and after the meeting. Such jobs included Greeters, Coffee Makers, people to help set up the room to assure all who attended had a place to sit. There were also such necessities as people who could hang up the banners, 12 steps and 12 traditions. Other jobs included people to take care of the inventory to assure the group could offer coffee and other such drinks. A person to take the minutes of business conducted meetings.

The meetings usually last one to one and a half hours, unless there were marathon meetings set for certain dates.

Every town and group had their own agenda as long as it conformed to the AA standards.

Certain topics were allowed and some did not conform to the policies set by each group.

People who wished to share on the topic and a five minute limitation was set to insure all who wanted to share were given an opportunity. The Board Members were comprised with any members with more than six months of uninterrupted sobriety.

The six month rule could be adjusted to one year if the Board voted the changes to apply, as soon as all the members were notified. The rest of the service work could also be adjusted according to the group's needs.

Service work outside of the group also had similar qualifications.

These Jobs included people who were willing to go to a prison to talk to the inmates or institutions that housed people with drinking problems and were trying to learn how to deal with these problems.

All of these jobs which were volunteer in nature and no money could be paid to those who responsibility these functions belong to. These jobs could last six months to one year.

These meetings fortunately came off with few problems if at all. The benefits of these meetings were designed to help as many people as possible. Each person who attended would take whatever story most applied to them, after all the intent was to show the similarities rather than the differences we as humans with a drinking problem have in common.

Phone lists were given out, so no one person would have to feel alone. They knew when to call for help and who was most likely to respond. We as Alcoholics can at any time recall what landed them in these rooms to begin with and what drinking alcohol could and would eventually do to such people. Honesty in its simplest terms seems to be easy up until you have to admit that you are an Alcoholic.

We as problem drinkers need to know there are numerous people who have the same disease we have and certainly are better able to understand the conversation that is being shared in and out of these rooms. They say no one came into these rooms on a winning streak. A bottom had been hit and for some more than one time. Now you may be able to see why I was instructed to attend these meetings, after all I was dying from living in denial. I would waste the first five months of attending meetings and sitting there in anger. That anger would soon be replaced with a new desire to take full advantage of my second chance to live a healthy and happy life.

I have held many different positions here in my home town and a town in close proximity of my home town.

There are other such functions within each AA group whether they are local in nature, regional or state wide.

The real consideration for those of us, whom are just getting started, is that AA does not close their doors to all that are seeking help. The belief is that if you are willing to learn a new way to handle your own personal problems without the usage of alcohol then AA can give you tools to utilize in dealing with them. Next you must come to understand, God is not just a religious belief, but rather spiritual in nature. I then tried a different part of AA. It is called H&I. This portion of the AA program has to deal with an individual going to a hospital with patients that have had medical damage caused by drinking alcohol. The "I" stands for institutions. These include prisons or jails that have alcoholics who are seeking a way to sobriety and a new life without alcohol. I decided to visit our prison system and assist in a three hour session in sharing with these people who had committed crimes while under the influence of alcohol or drugs or a combination of both of them.

I must admit I was terrified of walking through the prison yard with a bunch of men that had more tattoos than I had ever been surrounded by.

Once I entered the room where the sessions were to take place I became a little more comfortable. By the time the session was over I found out something about myself these men who were behind bars. I was fortunate not to be in there with them. I could have easily hurt innocent people while driving while under the influence. Learning this bit of information has helped me understand my disease and what I could do to help others with information that was given to me freely.

Once again GOD and AA has given me more tools to assist me in dealing with my new life and continue to find a new happiness that I would have never found any other way.

You must remember, AA does not say you will not have problems, but you will be given tools other than alcohol to attempt to correct these problems. I cannot be held responsible for a person who chooses to drink.

I must be prepared when a person comes to seek advice and assistance, rather than using the old stand-by line, I wish I had the time to help.

I can only hope that a person with this problem does not allow themselves to be that close to death before they seek help in rooms as the ones I have found.

These rooms are located everywhere in just about every town. Remember us as human have our flaws; sometimes it takes longer for some to see them. The only question becomes what would you be willing to do to find the solution the best fits your needs. As you will see, in my case it would take a near death experience on more than one occasion.

To conclude this portion of my story, I remembered when I first started to study the Big Book with my sponsor. He told me that he did not believe that I was going to live long enough or that I would not stay committed to the AA program for it to do me some good.

I must admit I had the same thoughts he did. As the story continues, we were proven wrong.

I believed my Higher Power had a lot to do with my staying committed to this program and that GOD himself was not ready for me to join him in the afterlife. I was starting to get a grasp on the 12 steps and the 12 traditions of the AA program. I was starting to become a different person, not only the way I was acting, but my thought process. I found myself volunteering for all kinds of functions within the AA program. People were starting to believe I was going to defeat my illness and I was going to be a good model roll for the new comers into the program.

I was starting to agree with them and found a new reason to smile.

# Chapter 4

Getting back to my personal story, seventeen days after being discharged from the hospital in San Francisco I would now be confronted with my first near death experience. It was approximately 9:00 pm on this particular evening. I had just said good-night to my friends and family that had come to visit me. I would not be prepared for what was about to occur at 1:00-2:00am.

Keep in mind I was waiting for death to come and take me for all eternity. I was not only scared but I recall that none of my family ever mentioned this topic when they were spending time with me.

As projected, the attack came to take me away in the early hours of the next morning. I do not recall what all occurred during this time, because my mind was put to sleep by my Liver, which had turned my contents inside my stomach to Ammonia. As far as we were able to piece the event that occurred, we came to the agreement the attack did not put me completely asleep.

When the attack happened I must have tried to get out of bed to seek assistance from my parents. I was able to lift myself up with the assistance of my walker. Unfortunately I had not locked the brakes, as I got up the chair took off without me and I was left to stand alone.

I must have tried to take a step and as I did I fell into my closet and landed on the bottom shelf face first. This would begin the start of a poisoned Liver Induced Coma. I would bruise my body and with a bit of luck, I had not done any damaged to my face or head. As far as I knew, I would have to be told what happened; first in my bedroom and what would happen in the emergency room at my favorite hospital were all of this had begun. I was informed of my problems. It was surmised that when the attacked hit me, I tried to get to my parents room. The fall had left my body bruised, but not as bad as my ego. Since I could not confirm as to my intentions were, I can only surmise these actions were most likely what I had intended to accomplish. My mother dialed 911 and told the emergency crew the address and what she knew had happened to her son.

After all she was the one who walked into my room and observed my waist and legs sticking out of the closet and no movement were visible. The Emergency crew arrived and after taking my vitals and asking my mother some pertinent questions I was lifted and carried to the ambulance and transported back to that little hospital.

The next thing I remember was waking up after what I thought was a peaceful night of sleep.

I would soon find out how wrong I was about my peaceful rest. The first thing I notice while wakening was the walls were so white and the room smelled of Lysol or a similar disinfectant. My sport banners, and other such sports items were missing from my walls.

The next thing that hit me was it was early in the morning and the sun's rays were coming through the window and was casting shadows on my floor. Who had put a window there? Since I was very familiar with my room setup I had no window where this window was. Now it became obvious to me what had happened. The attack had come and tried to take my life away from me.

For all I knew, I must be on my way to Heaven. The walls were white and everything seems to be so serene. After all if I was on my way to Hell, there would have been fire all over the place and the walls would have been red in color.

I also thought if this was indeed a down stairs movement, I would have been listening to some good Latin Music and someone should have been pouring me a shot of Tequila.

Since none of these were in my presence, I felt that Heaven was a few more seconds away. The next thing I noticed, there was an object sitting next to my hand.

I pushed what seems to be a buzzard. I heard nothing and thought it must be a silent alarm to inform GOD that I was awake and waiting to meet him. I began to focus my attention on the ceiling and having thoughts on what I would say to GOD when he came to introduce himself to me. The curtain to my left opened up, there staring down at me, was my angel, she was a Latina. She appeared to be in her mid-thirties, her smile was cute. I began to refocus on the ceiling, I had thoughts of thanking God for not only bringing me to Heaven, but also for including a angel that would be taking good care of me.

Now I only had one question that needed an answer. Since GOD and I had not officially met, was I going to be allowed to fool around with this angel or was it hands-off only?

Reality was once again about to slap me in the face. I turned to look back at my angel because she was clearing in throat and was about to inform me of my new surroundings. Instead, she had one question for me. Who the hell was I talking to? I then informed her that language like that was not to be used here and I was surprised the boss had let her get away with this type of language. She then asked me question number two, where did I think I was? I told her I did not see any gates, so this must be a waiting area for those who were awaiting their turn to enter Heaven. She then surprised me with the next bit of information she was about to enlighten me with.

I was on the third floor of my favorite hospital and she was the nurse on duty and she clarified one other item, her body was hands-off to me at all times.

So much for looking at the ceiling and assuming I was only having thoughts. I obviously must have been thinking rather loudly. The next set of questions seems to get more difficult to answer. She asked if I knew who was the Governor of our state was? I looked at her and asked, was she talking of the state of chaos. She answered no, she was asking about the state of California. I then replied, this state likes people from Hollywood, but I could not recall his name.

She then asked, if I knew who the President of our country was. I countered with, is he related to our Governor? She replied no. I was now 0 for 2. Ordinarily this would been an embarrassing moment, but instead I choose to chuckle and apologized for all that I had said. My nurse then informed me my doctor was on his way up to see me and clarified what had happened to me in the emergency room. My doctor entered my room and greeted me with a simple good-morning. He then informed me that my Liver had shut down my brain. This explained why I had no recollection of the chain of events that had landed me back in the hospital.

Turns out I was in a coma for a day and a half. I would spend the next four days under observation, and then my doctor paid me a visit to inform me that I was being released from his care and my medications were now altered to help prevent this from happening again. By this time my nurse and I were developing a healthier relationship. She was instrumental helping me out of bed and with walking. I was truly going to miss her and her cutting remarks that had been utilized to keep me in line.

As we said good-by she stated, I hope I never see you again.

I smiled at her as I was leaving my room. I thought to myself, certainly we had not spent enough time together for her to hate me already.

# Chapter 5

So I returned home and began to listen to my Care Giver who was a constant reminder what the doctor had said about taking all of the medications. In addition my food consumption and the times I would choose to consume them, so that I could get the correct nutritional food source and nutrients. At first I did what I was instructed to and all went better for me as far as keeping my contents in my stomach. This would last about a week, along with attending AA meetings with either my sister or mother close at hand. I still choose not to part take in any discussion these poor miss-informed people were sharing with each other. I knew I did not want anything they had to offer. With a closed mind, I learned absolutely nothing.

Then approximately two weeks after being discharged from the hospital, my parents found me once again unconscious at around 1:00 in the morning. This time I was draped over the bathtub rim and was clinging onto the shower curtain.

Once again I was in a poisoned liver induced coma and my mother dialed 911 and for the second time the emergency crew arrived and assisted I into their vehicle and off we went back to my new home away from home. This time when I awoke, I noticed my surroundings and knew where I was and had a good idea what had happened. Once again I pushed my buzzard and low and behold the same pretty Latina nurse strolled in with a smile on her face. It was all I could do without getting upset, I just rolled my eyes and looked at her and said, I knew where I was, on the third floor of my favorite hospital. The Governor was someone name Arnold and the President was someone named Bush.

This brought a bigger smile to her face and then she asked me if intended to make this a habit. I looked at her and started to laugh and she joined me. By the third day of my visit, I started to feel somewhat frustrated with this chain of events. After all I was no longer drinking or using drugs except for the correct prescription drugs the doctors had given me permission to use. I was no longer the life of any ones party and never felt so alone in my life. When my parents walked into my room, the conversation turned to going out with a bang. I informed my parents I was thinking about throwing a party for myself. I intended inviting all of my friends from San Diego, additionally and all of my friends who still were living in our small town. It was going to be a night of drinking and saying good-byes to all that would attend. If indeed I was going to check out, I wanted it to be on my circumstances. It was going to be a great night to remember, without having to wake the next day with a giant hangover. This thought did not go over real well with my mother. She refused to go along with this plan and asked me if I thought life was supposed to become easy? She went on to educate me on the importance of believing in God. I informed her that I did believe in God, but he was having trouble finding me and taking me to Heaven. All I was doing was making it easier for him to find my soul and start my adventure up to the Heavens above. She told me God did not work this way.

I would have to continue to fight to stay here on earth and do the best I could to be happy with the blessings that God had already been bestowed upon me. I did notice my nurse was starting to come in and check on me a little more frequent, than before. I was wrapped up into my problems and feeling sorry for myself I really did not notice a lot of the little things that were happening around me.

Our conversations turned into sharing of information on our families, both good and bad. We found a mutual respect for each other and I knew I had found a new friend I could share some of my most secretive stories I had never shared before.

My doctor, who was assigned to look in on me from time to time by the hospital, came in to visit with me and she asked me what I wished to do about finding a new Liver Transplant hospital or did I want to keep the same one in San Francisco. I informed him, I would not be returning to that particular establishment and I needed to find a new hospital. Preferably one that did not categorize me as a person who slept under an underpass or in an alleyway. After all I wasn't one of those people you see walking around with a plain brown bag. He told me the best approach on this matter and that he would be able to make an appointment with my doctor.

He was the doctor that had sent me to that first hospital. I had some unkind words saved up for him. I was released from my hospital after five days of observation, my medications once again had been adjusted and like a routine, I went home with my parents and started anew once again. I did make another appointment with my doctor and we sat and started to develop a new plan.

Meanwhile we also had numerous comments on whose local sports teams would fare better on the upcoming year.

I was also informed on my monthly out of pocket expense my medications were costing me. After all I had gone from paying 10.00 a month on my medication to help me with my diabetes, to 500.00 for all the new medications that had been introduced to me for my current condition.

I was still having problems with gaining weight. Every time I thought about only weighing 140lbs. I thought how many times I had tried to lose weight, but could never stay committed and soon the weight would return.

This way of losing weight was not exactly what I had in mind, but it was certainly nothing I had to make a commitment to. We were now in the middle of March of 2008. I had been in two different hospitals and was searching for a third. I had gone from someone who had never been to a hospital, to a person who was now seeking out one that I could be comfortable with. Not just with the doctors and nurses, but for a hospital that was clean and disinfected properly.

We would soon found such a hospital in the months to come. You must remember up until these set of incidents happened to me, I had not spent one day or night in any type of hospital.

Some people are hard to please; I like to think I do not fall into this category. I just want to be treated with respect and wanted to make relatively sure the hospital was kept cleaned and germs were kept down to a minimum. I did not want another infection to invade my sickly body.

The last one was quite sufficient in teaching me infections did not have a positive effect on me.

# Chapter 6

*My return home would not be a long stay. On the third night I had been released from my hospital, I had said good night to all who were there. It was starting to get to be fun seeing all my nephews and other relatives.*

*For some reason I was in some pain in my stomach and could not find a comfortable spot to start a long recovering sleep. On this particular evening my parents had taken their go to sleep medication and both were in deep sleep and as I would find out later. Around 12:00 midnight the pain had grown considerable and I started to feel as a trip to the hospital once again would soon be at hand. I tried to wake my mother, but did not have any luck calling out her name, so she could waken to assist me in my current dilemma. When she did not respond, I decided to go to plan B. I used my cell phone and called my parents, knowing they had a phone answering machine in their room. I heard the voice recorder come on a waited for the beep. I did my best to cry out for help, but neither one of my parents was responding. I decided to go to my next plan. I called my care giver who lived maybe three blocks away. She answered and queried what was wrong. I told her about my growing pain in my stomach and I thought the best thing for me to do was go to the hospital. I then told her about my parents and she responded that she would be there to assist me within ten minutes.*

*I hung up and sat up in my bed and my stomach felt like it was full of big stones wanting to escape in any way possible. I then made a major mistake, after getting partly dressed I tried to stand up on the far side of the bed using the wall as leverage. I took one step forward and began to fall. I could see the dresser coming at my head, but could do nothing to stop my forward movement. My bad luck was about to change. On my way down I hit the side of the bed and body was deflected in a sideward movement and I hit the wall first and then come to rest on the floor just* short of the dresser. The pain was felt so strong and bad I felt tears rolling down my eyes. Then the thought hit me, what if I had hit the dresser instead? I started to thank GOD for my luck change. Bad luck was not all the way gone though, when my care giver tried to use her key to come into the house, she found quickly that my mother had locked the dead bolt, which neither of us had a duplicate key for this lock. She knocked on the door and as I would have predicted, there was no response from either one of my parents. My care giver noticed my parents' bedroom window was open, so without hesitating she went to the open window and started calling out my mom's name. At first there was no response, although I could hear her. Finally my mother awoke and she wondered who was calling her name. She found out quickly, she got out of her bed and went to the front door to let my care taker in. They both came to my room and saw me lying face down and rushed to my side and asked me if I was still awake, I answered yes, but was in a lot of pain. They lifted me up and sat me back on the bed and finished dressing me. Now I am headed back for the turned out to be the biggest nightmare trip and stay at my favorite hospital. The trip that only took 15 minutes, was not only painful, but every bump on the road seem to grow in intensity as far as bring me a new level of pain.

We finally arrived and my care giver, whom was now becoming a pro at getting me into the hospital, wheeled me in and the waiting room to see a doctor. This room was full of young and old alike, all with a different degree of pains and aches. I noticed there was an elderly man sitting in the waiting room and he needed an oxygen tank and mask. I remembered thinking I was so glad I was not in his current condition.

The young man checking people in and taking their vitals called me to come join him at his station. After getting his questions answered and checking my vitals, he told me I would have to go back to the waiting room and wait my turn. I informed him that would not be a good idea since my stomach was now letting me know I was going to be rather sick in quick fashion.

I asked him if he could just find me a pillow and let me lay down in the hallway next to a garbage can I would try and make do. He replied that was against hospital regulations and there was no place for me to lie down. Keep in mind when they wheeled me in, the waiting room was full and nothing had changed on my return back to this room. I was sitting there talking to my mother and care giver for about 5 minutes, when I looked at them both and told them to get away from me. They both looked at me and began to move.

At which time I began to make that little girl from the movie Exorcist seem like an amateur when it came to how quickly and how far projectiles coming from my stomach could fly. Where hers was green in color, mine was a nice mixture of red blood and hint of everything I had put in my stomach earlier that day. I was given a trash can half way through this episode, but the mess I would leave behind; well I think you get the general idea. Within a few moments the young man who had checked my vitals was coming out the door calling my name.

My mother turned me around so I could see him and responded with I am here and that I was still alive. He then told me I was next and he began to wheel me into the Emergency Area.

I inquired about the rest of the people waiting; he said it was my turn. As I turned to look at the once filled waiting room, I couldn't help but notice all of the people had relocated to the sidewalk outside. I really felt bad for the older man who needed an oxygen tank, just to breathe. He was standing out there looking in. I was wheeled into the Emergency Room and laid on a bed, with the help of a pretty young nurse. She greeted me with a hello and used my first name. I asked if she knew me and she informed me, she had taken care of me on my two prior visits to the Emergency Room. She then turned around and called out to two people passing by.

The first young lad was a male nurse and the second one was his aide. This older man was a well groomed Chinese individual. He was a nice talking and very cordial man. She looked at both of them and said look who has come back for a visit. They greeted me and said it was time I was awake to meet those who had been taking care of me.

She started to set up an "IV" bottle of liquid and hung it from this "IV" Holder. While she was doing this task, up walked the doctor and introduced himself to me and he used my first name like he knew who I was. Needless to say the emergency team was now in place and they all knew me and my condition and were waiting for further instructions from the doctor. I was having a real problem with breathing and I was struggling with forming words and trying to talk. The first question he would ask me was what had brought me in this time? I tried to tell about stomach and the pain I was in. He then felt my stomach and looked at the nursed and instructed her to start the "IV". It turned out to be a pain killer and then looked back at me and said he need to leave, but that he would return in 5 minutes. He did instruct my care giver not to give me anything to drink. While he was gone my tongue and throat became very dry, so I asked my care giver to wet a paper towel so I could place it in my mouth. She complied and continues this series of events while acting like a look out, watching for the return of the doctor. When he did return, he was not alone, he had a young intern with him and informed me this person had experience with than he did with this problem. He started to explain to me, my Liver had completely shut down and my stomach was full of fluid. He was not sure what had caused it, but knew what the solution was. He then told me he was going to insert a tube and needle into my stomach right above bellybutton.

He would first have to give me another shot of pain killers at the point of insertion. What he needed to know from me, when I felt my stomach feel warm to hot, this would indicate to him that the medication was working.

This would not take long and I thought the problem had been corrected.

He then informed me, he was going to insert a metal tube into my stomach, because the fluid had to be drained out.

He went on to say, he would need me to be conscious for this particular procedure. He then instructed my care giver to grab my head and turn it toward her. He began to insert the tube and even with the shot in my stomach which was meant to deaden the surrounding area, the pain was very noticeable. As he was inserting the tube, he looked at the intern and asked him about the angel of the tube and the intern informed him he was going to the mark. The doctor told my care giver to release my head and as I turned to look at him, he told me he was going to have to remove the tube and try again. He went on to say this was going hurt more than the first attempt. He inserted the tube for the second time and the pain was brutal. As what would become my reaction to this kind of pain, I let the doctor know what I thought of him and his family.

Once again he looked at the intern and this time the intern informed him, he was on target. The doctor asked the intern how much they were going to drain, 1 or 2. I asked 1 or 2 what and before the doctor could answer the intern answered more like 4 or 5. The doctor had a surprised look on his face and once again I inquired what they were talking about. The doctor told me they were going to drain 4-5 liters of liquid from my stomach. All I could do was picture the liters soft drinks came in. I don't know about you, but this certainly seemed like a lot of fluid.

Especially from someone who weighed all of 140 pounds.

The intern then explained he was ready to insert the syringe into the part of my stomach were the tube was resting. The doctor told him to release the fluid and I looked at the bag and watched it start to fill with a mixture of clear and red fluid.

The doctor then informed us that he was needed to go and treat an older man they had just brought in. He told the intern to stay and monitor the drainage. That intern nodded his head as to indicate he would comply with the doctor's request.

The first time the bag was filling, the intern and I would carry conversations on topics that included drinking and other abusive drugs. He then stopped the drainage to change bags. This intern went on to inform me that each of the bags could hold two liters of fluid. On the final bag the syringe automatically popped on its own and the intern said that all of the fluid now out of my stomach. He went to find the doctor and they returned together. The doctor gave me the next step that would be occurring. This turned out to be further bad news. He had called the X-Ray Tech and he was on his way up to take two pictures of my stomach. I looked up at my doctor and said that did not sound so bad. He informed me, the position the Tech was going to put me in was the painful part. I was told that if I did what was being asked of me, this procedure would be over in thirty seconds. The way he should have worded this, was it only going to take 30 seconds, but it will feel like an eternity.

In walked the X-Ray Tech and asked if I was ready, I looked at him and I said if you do not get this right the first time, I would not give him a second chance. He began to put me in the position he needed me to be in.

I let out a scream and may have said something about his mother. He got the two pictures and left, my doctor returned with another doctor. This doctor asked me, what medication I was taking for my diabetes. I answered and he countered with do not take that medication anymore, it was destroying my Liver. Then my doctor advised me that this was going to be at least a 9 day stay for me. When I awoke the next morning in my room up on the third floor, you could not guess who was waiting for me to waken? I looked up at her with my enduring smile and said good-morning; she responded with, she was still married, so a date with her was still out of the question. When bad luck is the only luck you have, you can prepare yourself a lot better when you get this information.

In walked my doctor and he started to lay out all they were going to do me. I was going to get a complete blood transfusion, which included Platelets, anti-bio tics, a salt solution and of course the new blood. He went on to tell me I would get a chance to see my family the next day.

My nurse came in the next day to inform me my family was on their way up and she was going to go and talk to them before they would be allowed to see me. A couple of minutes later in walked my mom and dad first. My mom took one look at me and shook her head and walked out of my room. My father was sitting on his walker and had a blank look on his face. In walked my younger sister and when she looked at me, she shook her head and asked if I had seen myself? I answered with a simple no.

She then asked me, if I remember the old movie when Boris Karloff played the part of Frankenstein. I said yes, she responded with I looked like him when they were rising him to meet the electrical storm. My father simply smiled and nodded with agreement of my sister's assessment. I asked her if she had a mirror and she answer sure. She positioned her mirror so that I could see the pole to my left. I soon saw what she meant, I had four bags of red and clear liquid pouring into arm. She then walked around the bed and showed me my right side; it was identical as my left side. I thought that this was a lot of liquid pouring into my system at one time. Then my sister showed me my head.

I had a bunch of censors attached to my head and there job was to monitor the beeping that was going on behind my head. My father was at shaking his head in disbelief. I stayed that way for a day and a half, when they came to start unhook me from the needles, my arms were bruised considerably. It took an additional four more days for what turned out to be a double infection that attacked my body. On the seventh day I was allowed to sit up in my bed and have some breakfast.

A therapist walked in and informed me she was here to help me to balance myself along with learning to walk again with my walker.

By the end of the eighth day my doctor told me I could go home the next day. This was by far one of the most memorable and painful visits I would endure. When they released me, my nurse came up to me and said, she was getting tired of taking care of me. I asked her how she had been so unlucky to have to take care of me every time.

She informed me, when she came in the morning, she went through the Emergency Ward to see if I had returned and if I had, she would have herself assigned to my ward and room. I started to laugh and told her, I knew this was not luck of the draw. Then I turned to walk over to my wheelchair, I truly knew she really did care about me.

# Chapter 7

When I got home, I must admit I was now feeling the weakest I had ever felt. As I ready myself to get back into my bed, it was now April and I was still alive. After all, I was given only 30 days to live in mid-January. I started to wonder if indeed, some one was playing a hoax and I was the last one to be told about it. Then I asked myself the question I had refused to allow myself to think about in the last week or so. Was I living on borrowed time?

Up until this time I had attended nine AA meetings and still was running in the silent mode. My mind was still closed to hearing of the truth and I was standing by my first thought.

These people attending these meetings had nothing to offer me. I couldn't help but wonder, was this test given to Liver patients to see if they were willing to do whatever it took to get a new Liver. After a couple of days of rest, my energy level started to improve and I started getting back up to have my meals and to visit with the people that would stop by to visit.

I was really feeling a lot better overall and I was eating and enjoying my food. Well Cinco DE Mayo came and went and I had completed one year of sobriety. I was happy that I had survived the initial disaster of my bad health and my body falling apart.

I really did start to believe that I was living on borrowed time. Two weeks had gone by since my last stay at the hospital, and then once again death came knocking on my door at around 2:00am. As to what happened to me, that is something I will never know. I had a hard time trying to figure what my intent was when the attack happened. All I know is my dad came into my room somewhere around 3:00 and turned on my bedroom light and saw me lying face down on the floor and for all appearances I was no longer alive. My dad said he bent down to touch me and I was as cold and stiff as an icicle which hung from one of our eaves. My dad thought the worst had happened, but he covered me up with a blanket.

My father was a man who fought in the Korean Conflict and then went on to be a butcher in a major slaughter house. He had never gotten emotional in front of me when I was a kid. He was raised a traditional Hispanic man who was raised with the belief, men did not show their emotions. The more my dad looked at me, he thought the best thing he could do was wrap me in a warm blanket.

I would be told later that my dad had broken down with tears. My mother walked in and dialed that number she had dialed many times before and set the emergency crew into action.

The following like the two other coma episodes is a recreation through the eyes of my parents and the EMT; S. When the emergency crew got there they tried to get a temperature reading, but all they got from there digital read out was Error. The man in charged then instructed one of the other members of the crew, to go to the truck and get all the warm blankets from the heating bin they were in. They ended up wrapping me into five of those blankest, but as far as they knew I was pretty much history. If I was breathing it was very shallow, but the heart rate was nonexistent.

Once the blankets were on me for a couple of minutes, I let out a breath of air and once again they tried to get another reading, this time the thermometer read 92.6 degrees. My breathing had returned and my heart rate was coming up. They thought this would be the best time to load me in the truck and get me to the hospital. They told me I ended up staying in the Emergency Room a longer time than the previous visits.

Now in the following paragraphs, you can draw your own conclusions as to what happened. These part wholes true today as much it as it did when this incident occurred.

Something happened to me that would change my life.

I was raised a Catholic, but never went to church after I left to join the Air Force. I did believe in GOD, but I had been so mad at him for so long for all of the failures I had had in my personal life. I was not ready to forgive him so easily. I had been asleep for a couple of days, when I began to awaken. As I woke up I could hear the speaker outside of my door, calling for some nurse to come to a certain room. Then as if they had been standing there for a while, I heard two doctors talking about my health and weather I was going to recover. I tried to open my eyes to get a look at them, but my eyes lids would not open.

So I continue to listen to the two doctors and the one closest to me said, there was no way I was going to recover from this attack. Then the second doctor spoke. He said as he spoke to the other doctor, you are so wrong, here read these pages. What does this sentence mean, the first one questioned. The second doctor went on to say, this man has not yet finished his work. He still yet to do any of these items listed here. Now I gave my eyes one more chance to open and could not get them to respond. So I reached over and grabbed my buzzard and waited for my nurse to enter.

I could hear her talking just outside of my door, and then the two doctors decided it was time for them to leave.

Next thing I heard was my curtain being pulled on and I heard the voice of my favorite nurse call out my name (I was unaware she had been off for the last two days) as she was asking me if I was truly awake. I replied with, unless she had seen GOD in my room, it was me who had ringed that buzzard. Then I informed her I could not open my eyes. She informed me to keep them closed and she would take care of the problem. I heard her go into my restroom and run some water and then she returned to my side. She began to wipe my eyes with a hot wet towel. A few moments later she said OK open your eyes. As I did my eyes were out of focus and I couldn't make out to much of what or who was in my room. My nurse told me my eyelashes had been glued together by that crust that forms in the corner of your eyes sometimes when you sleep real deep. She asked how I felt and I told her I was a bit tired but over all I was doing okay.

She did not hesitate in telling how close I was to dying and the work they had done to save me in the Emergency Room took quite a long time and they knew it would be touch and go for a while. When she first arrived and inquired about my status, she was briefed by the on duty nurse that all was not going well for me. She said she had come in earlier to take a look at me and I was as pale and weak as she ever remembered seeing me.

When I rang my buzzard, she was surprised I was awake and could move enough to summon her to my room. I then asked her a questioned that got her off guard. I inquired about the two doctors who were talking about my case and I was wondering who they were. She looked down at me and said she was going to check on my doctor's arrival to my room. She would return a few minutes later with a clipboard in her hand and advised me my doctor was on the way up and would be here in about 5 minutes. I replied with I would like to have steak and eggs for breakfast. She turned around and just smiled as she left.

When she returned, I once again inquired about the two doctors, this time when she looked down at me, she asked me a question. She asked me how many times I had been here before. I responded this was my fourth time, and I looked up at her to see she was not smiling. I asked her if anything was wrong and she answered, no. She then asked me the next question, was I familiar with the hospital policy for doctors who were coming to see a patient. I answered yes, that they had to check in with her and then sign in on a form that she kept attached to a clipboard (like the one she was holding in her hand).

The information contained on this form, was times in and out of the rooms along with who they were visiting and why. She then showed me the clipboard she was holding and the forms were empty. Once again I looked up at her and she informed me no one had been up to see me this morning. She continued to tell me the drugs they had administered me while I was in the Emergency Room could cause me to hallucinate.

I agreed with her and never again broached this subject with her again. I knew what I heard and I only wished I would have been able to open my eyes at the time.

My family came to visit me and it consisted of my mom and dad. My mother started as usual to feel me in on what had occurred and then my father spoke. As he began to tell me what he had seen, he started to cry, telling me he thought I was dead. When he had bent down to touch me, he said there was no signs of life and he started crying then. I assured him I was alright and be home as soon as I could to continue living. The next occurrence that would happen to me, I yet to try to figure out what it all meant. I was lying in my bed one morning and in walked my doctor with another doctor I had never seen before. He asked me a few questions and then he asked me the most serious one of them all. He wanted to know, how bad did I want that surgery for my Gall Bladder? I knew this, I was tired of getting sick and not am able to consume food that use to bring me so much pleasure. I asked him, why these questions were being asked? He said he was the doctor who was willing to do the surgery to remove my Gall Bladder and all of the stones that were lodged into my stomach. He said he would give me a few moments to think about it and then he would return for my answer.

Keep in mind the surgery was scheduled to take place the next morning if I told him yes. So my care giver and I talked it over and came to the conclusion that I wanted that organ out of me. In walked my parents and we informed them what had happened and the first to speak was my mom. She wanted to know where this doctor had come from and why was he willing to do the surgery no other doctor would consider doing? The two doctors returned as promise and my parent saw him for the first time. My mother, who is very religious, took an instant dislike to this particular doctor. She then informed the two doctors that we would need a little more time.

They walked back out and my mom turned to me and said rather abruptly, that she was not in favor of allowing this doctor to conduct the surgery and that waiting until I got better was a much better plan. I replied with, she was not the one in pain. After all I was to the Emergency Room enough times to become real tired of my home away from home.

In walked the two doctors and we informed them we were going to wait until another time. They responded with they would remain at the hospital and if I had a change mind, they would set up the surgery times. My doctor came in to visit and set the tone of the seriousness of this particular attack had been and the toll that it had taken on me. I would end up spending 7 days in the hospital this time around.

I met with a nutritionist and she laid out a diet that would be easy for me to follow. The doctors made one more adjustment to my medication and then told me I was ready to be discharged. My doctor had also indicated that I would probably not survive another attack. I responded with he need not worry about another attack. I was not going to return to this hospital in this condition again. He then asked, if I planned to end my life. I answered with no, I was going to go home and get healthy.

I was preparing myself to leave the hospital once again.

My family came in and I told them I had a new lease on life.

They just looked at me as if they could not figure what I meant.

On the fifteen minute drive home, I kept replaying what the voices had said. What work had I not done? Since that part was never discussed I was doing my best to figure what work I had left to do. When we did return home my mother called my local doctor and told her what had occurred at the hospital. My doctor's first response was this doctor serious and was HE CRAZY? My mother assured her this had happened and my doctor informed her, that we had made a good decision, because I was not ready physically ready for surgery and my vitals were not completely in line for such a procedure. Then the doctor asked my mother, where had this doctor and where did he come from? No answer was forthcoming.

I must admit I was just confused as my doctor was and I knew I was still getting very sick and I was growing tired of running to the bathroom. I wanted to gain weight and help myself become more stable as far as my daily vitals were concerned. My care giver and I were becoming a better team as far as medication and food consumption. My life was in such array and free fall, I was looking for every angle I could find to help myself.

**I THOUGHT FOR A MOMENT AND CAME UP THIS QUESTION. WAS THIS MY FIRST MEETING WITH GOD AND HAD I RESPONDED TO HIM CORRECTLY?**

**THEN ANOTHER QUESTION CAME TO ME. WAS MY THINKING PROCESS JUST ANOTHER WAY OF TRYING TO BULLSHIT MYSELF?**

**After all I had become rather good at this particular method of thinking my way through life. WHAT IF TRULY THIS WAS A VISIT FROM MY HIGHER POWER. WAS I GOING TO BE TRUE TO MY WORDS, TO CHANGE MY WAYS?**

# Chapter 8

I had been home for a couple of days and I had nothing on my mind except what I had heard. I knew on this evening there was an AA meeting as usual. I got myself ready to go and my mother walked in, and said what are you doing? I looked at her and responded, I am going to the AA meeting. I went on to inform her; I no longer needed assistance in getting ready or driving myself to the meeting. I walked into the meeting and sat down. The meeting started and ended as usual except this time when the meeting was about to conclude, I raised my hand and stood up and said the following information I stated my name, I am an ALCOHOLIC and I need someone to teach me what is inside of this Big Book" This room we were sitting in was carpeted, but you could have heard that needle hit the floor. What were so surprising to me were the people who were in attendance looks on their faces. They were all staring at me and most of them had a chin that has dropped rather noticeably.

This man stood up and gave me his number and told me to call him. So began my education into the world of "AA" and let me tell you, I knew nothing about this particular subject. I was doing okay with going to this man's house and he began from the beginning on the transition into the world of "AA".

I was not really paying attention to what he said, because I was caught up with selection of sports memorabilia. You see I am an Oakland Raider, Los Angeles Dodgers and Los Angeles Lakers fan. This man was a San Francisco 49er, San Francisco Giant and Sacramento kings fan. I looked up to the heavens and asked, what does this man and I have in common, except for our drinking problem? I then thought my GOD has a unique sense of humor. When our meeting concluded I had a better understanding of what I was to expect. **Not only from my new sponsor, but what would be expected of me.** All was going well with my health and then a small attack hit me and did not completely drop me into a coma, but it did put my mind to sleep with ammonia poison. It was about the two week mark of my release from the hospital, when around 6:00am. This time my mom walked into my bedroom and she could see me sitting on the edge of the bed rocking back and forth. She turned on my light and wished she hadn't. I had gotten sick all over, my bed and my bedroom floor. She told me later that day that I was responding to her questions, but my answers were not making any sense.

She called my care giver and she said she would be there in a few minutes. Between the two, they were able to get me undressed, cleaned up and dressed again.

My adopted brother walked in on his way to eat breakfast and he stopped to say hello and to check on me. The ladies had gotten me dressed, so they asked my adopted brother to help me to the car. I could walk, but I could not see anything because my brain had shut down again. We got to my SUV and my brother opened the passenger door to the back seat and asked if I needed some help getting in and putting on my seat belt.

I responded I did not need any further assistance. He stood there watching me and then a few moments later he asked me if I was going to get into my SUV? I responded with, what are you a comedian? I am seated and have my seat belt on.

He then knew it was time to put me in the vehicle and put my belt on and the four of us were off and running to, you guessed it, the hospital. As to what happened in the emergency room that morning, I all I have to go on like a good portion of this story, is what I was told happened. At around 10:00am this particular morning, I woke up and the first thing I noticed was my emergency nurse who was seated next to bed. As I turned towards her I said good-mourning and she looked up at me and was surprised to see me looking at her. The first thing she said was, she could not believe I was awake already. I asked how long had I been there and she responded about three and a half hours.

She then began to inform me what all had happened since my arrival. She said I had come in yelling and screaming at everyone.

When they moved me onto the bed and put the oxygen hose up my nose, I fought with the male nurse and his aide.

I then pulled the hose completely out of my nose and started to bleed from both nostrils. The male nurse tried to restrain me and I threw a right cross at him. The Chinese male nurse aide went from being Chinese and a man I had come to know and have great respect for on prior visits to being a Japanese Kamikaze pilot who was responsible for taking to a lot of Americans out at Pearl Harbor.

My mother who was standing there watching all this happened came to my side and tried to calm me down.

I started in on her and told she should go back to the movie "The Wizard of OZ" and grab her broom and fly off.

Needless to say this really hurt my mother and the doctor told her I did not know what I was saying and who I was saying it to. I then broke out in Spanish and continued the verbal assault on my mom. They finally got the "IV" hooked up and put me to sleep. Now that I was awake, my nurse noticed the two men who were trying to restrain me. She called them both over and I said hello, I then tried to explain to the two men, my female nurse had filled me in and I am truly sorry for my actions and my vocabulary usage earlier that morning.

The male nurse walked up to me and said, that I could really throw a mean right hand and it was he could do to duck out of the way. We laughed about it and the Chinese man walked up to me and asked if I remembered who he was? I answered yes and I knew he was not at Pearl Harbor. Once again we broke out in laughter. Then the male nurse asked if I had seen my mother and my female nurse answered and said my mom and my care giver were in the Cafeteria having coffee. In walked my care giver and the three of my helpers excused themselves and said good luck. My care giver started to inform me what was said in the cafeteria with my mom. I told her I knew what I had said and done and needed to see my mother. She said that would not be a problem, she was on her way back from the cafeteria. I asked my care giver what had happened at the house and she started laughing as she started to tell me the parts she knew to be true. As she was telling me this story I heard a knock on the wall and it was the hand belonging to my mom. She stepped around the corner and I said good morning to her and she replied, you know who I am? I said yes, you are my mom. I told her I was sorry the crew had told me what had happened and I told her I would have had better start of my day if the attack had left me unconscious.

Then my doctor walked in and said good-morning, and how was I feeling? I told him my nostrils hurt and could he please wire my mouth shut. He then said that they were going to send me upstairs for a brief stay I said okay and they prepared me for my trip once again to the third floor.

Once in my room and saying hello to everyone on the third floor, I fell asleep and slept for the rest of the day. The next morning they sent a female in to draw 6 tubes of blood from me, so they could see the damage done. Then my doctor came in and we both had a good laugh about me being back once again. I would be released the following day and the early reports were not as bad as he thought they might be.

The next morning my doctor came in and said I was released and I thanked him. He then told me once again.

That one more severe attack and I were probably not going to survive this time. We both smiled and I said this is my final good-by. This would be the last time I saw my favorite third floor nurse. I am truly sorry I could not find the proper words to tell her how much her company and aid had made to this tired old man. This was one of the first times in a long while, I felt truly blessed to have a great group of people in the Emergency Room and the properly trained third floor employees.

I WOULD CERTAINLY MISS ALL OF THOSE WONDERFUL PEOPLE THAT ASSISTED ME SO MANY TIMES AND SO WELL!!!!

# Chapter 9

I kept thinking about what had happened to me while I was coming out of this last coma. The two voices were very persistent and would not allow me to forget what had taken place. As the situation kept replaying itself in my mind, I could not help but start to figure a way to explain what couldn't be explained logically. The fact of the matter was, I wasn't one hundred percent on all that had happened and what it truly meant to me. What I did come up with, I worked 26 years for the federal government and the hardest work I had ever done was to find a way not to work.

What I had learned in my AA lesson plans was that if I didn't believe what I was being taught, that faking it was the best solution. The reason for such thinking was to help my sponsor to continue to enrich my education process so that I would not delay further information from being processed. Meanwhile I was getting healthier and stronger, which aided in my continue involvement with the AA process. I went to a neighboring town and sat in one of their meetings.

I met some good people and they invited me to join their group as a volunteer.

For the first time I was having fun doing tasks that I would Have never had done in the past. Slowly but surely, I started to realize my story was very similar to the stories being shared in these meetings. I only hoped I would be able to perform these new duties in a manner that showed my sincerity of my newly developed education.

As I continue on, we are in June of 2008. Something had become very clear to me, I was living day to day and not giving to much thought for my future. I wanted to live for some years to come, but I was not sure what the future was to bring me. Nothing had really changed in my ailments, truth be known, the only change was my new belief in a higher power and my attitude.

What thought came next to me was about to make itself apparent. I started to recall the past and all of those whose lives I may have touched both positively and negatively.

Forcing me to try to remember all of those whom may have been innocent, but stood before me and fell within the wrath I was handing out on any given night. I managed to have four LOVE relationships. These would not last for a long time, except for my marriage which lasted ten years.

The fourth woman I would be involved with was in my mind, the last relationship I would ever need. That would last for twelve years on and off because of the distance that separated us.

In these next chapters to come, I will try to explain why these love relationships failed at that time. More importantly, not only why they failed, now that my mind has now been somewhat cleared without the usage of alcohol and other drugs. The one thing I have found out is the burden I must carry for these damages. Not only was I guilty of cruelty and ego based belittlement.

I truly thought at the time I was innocent of any wrong doing, everyone else was at fault. The rest of my list contains my immediate family and all of my friends and the friends of the women who had a relationship with me. All these people at one time or another been present while I was so busy trying to rule the world. There were also the people who just passed my way while I was drinking. They were guilty of one thing, being in my presence when I was telling the rest of the world what their problems were and how to correct them. To say that all that knew me were tolerant of my behavior doesn't begin to describe what each of them must have restrained themselves from saying. The language and the intent of the words coming from my mouth were not kind and not said with much respect for anyone feelings. Do not get the wrong impression, when my family came to visit me, I made sure that all would be taken care of. I would take them to my favorite spots in Baja California and pay for the food and entertainment. I wanted my family to know how important there happiness was to me.

# Chapter 10

Now has come the time for me to share with you, my personal life and how it correlates with my career choice I made when I joined the USAF. I married a young lady that I met while in the last part of my senior year of High School.

While I was dating her I graduated and left to become a Chef in the USAF. While I was at basic training at Lackland AFB in San Antonio, TX. My selection of careers came to an abrupt halt. I was advised the Air Force no longer needed Chefs. I was given the option of taking an Honorable Discharge or accept this new job in a field I knew nothing about. I knew nothing of the aviation field, but was assured the Air Force would teach me all I needed to know to do the job. I truly wanted to get my military time out of the way and I did not want to go home.

I opted to stay in the and was sent to Air Force and accept there new school and job offer. This school was located in Biloxi, Mi. For my school and the beginning of my training to do a job I would have never thought I would be capable to do. You must remember I was from a small town and knew very little about the world. On my first day at Biloxi I was educated about the southern states and some of the differences I was about to come face to face with.

To say these people took prejudice to a new level does not begin to describe the awakening that was very open and very violent. That aside, I successfully completed the training program and was told my next base was located in New Mexico. My alcohol consumption grew while I was in Biloxi. I started out a beer drinker, but by the time I left, I was consuming all kinds of alcohol. At twenty one I had been drinking for five years. I was still dating he same young lady. We would get married while I was in New Mexico and all went well until I served my four years and was discharged from the Air Force. Our next stop for us was the State of Texas.

I would not fare so well in this State. I was fired from a job because I choose to treat my employees like people, instead of the way my employers wanted me to. We came back home to the town we had grown up in. Our marriage was falling apart and I asked my ex-wife for a divorce, but she wanted to work our problems out. This is what she told me, in my opinion, what she meant was she was pregnant, but wasn't yet showing.

In 1981, our President of the made a bold decision and move that would attack the Federal Government jobs that had Union affiliation. The job I was doing at the time when this occurred was nothing to brag about.

Meanwhile my ex-wife had given birth to my son and even though he was small and sickly, he was still a very energetic and a handful of a little guy.

I decided to apply for the government job that had become available and was hire in August of 1982. I reported to Palm Springs and began my training at my new facility, but a job I knew so well. I was now doing a different style of my past employment while in the Air Force. I knew nothing of identifying civilian aircraft and indeed I couldn't tell the difference between a Bonanza and a Cessna or for that matter the difference between a B737 and a MD80. I made it through the Tower Portion of my training and was informed I needed to go the Oklahoma to the Academy to further my education of working in the civilian capacity.

I successfully completed and graduated from the Academy. I called my ex-wife and she advised me she was setting up one hell of a return for me on my return from Oklahoma. When I returned and walked into my duplex, the first thing I noticed was it was completely empty.

There was a letter sitting on the kitchen counter, I read it and was informed by my ex-wife, she had taken my son and our belongings and moved back home to the north central part of our state.

We would divorce two years later and while I was still in training at my job, I was then told I had failed the training program. I was offered a job in the San Diego area. Needless to say my consumption of alcohol was starting to increase to a level that should have been a warning to me.

I reported to my new airport and successfully completed the training program. I began to venture out in my social life and found a young lady and we began to date. She was 7 years younger than me and had just broken up with a young man she had been dating. We met at an establishment I would drink and eat dinners at. I bought an alcoholic drink and later that night, I bought her dinner and we continued our casual conversation. I gave her my number and told her to call me if she needed someone to talk to. She called a couple of days later and we went out again, she expressed that she was tired of the way she had been treated by her selection of men. We started to date and she began to express feelings for me and we were having an enjoyable time together. Then along came a young man she knew in High School and my company was no longer needed.

The last year I would spend at this facility, I met a lady who drove the City Buses. We became close and through our dating process, she asked me to move in with her. She was already buying a home, so I moved in and all went well. On the fifth month of living together,

her mother got sick and needed care. I was asked to move out, so my ex-girlfriend could take care of her mother's needs.

After completing four years of working as a tower controller, I was on my way upstairs to report for work. I passed my bosses office and he called for me to step into his office and I complied. He advised me a facility 45 minutes north of my present facility had called and needed help.

He advised me I was to report there on the following Monday. I did not want to go and was very happy where I was working. I was not given an option. I reported to my new facility and I knew I was going to struggle to make this training program.

I had failed at Palm Springs and this facility was a much larger facility than that and the responsibilities were so much bigger. I was not only going to work traffic into and out of Orange County Airports, I was going to help traffic flow to all parts of Southern California as well as traffic with destinations worldwide.

This was going to be the toughest job I was going to have to succeed at during my FAA career.

My drinking beer now was a part of my past and I was consuming nothing but hard alcohol. It did not matter whether it was Tequila, Rum or Vodka. It was now a matter of reaching the intoxication level I was in search of.

I was a social drinker and sometimes I was called a power drinker. I never thought for a moment, was I drinking so much? I concluded the thought with; I was trying to fit in my surroundings.

My son would come to live with me while I was living in Orange County and we were happy together.

We would spend a lot of time at the amusement and sports parks that Southern California had to offer. We would also attend a good many concerts and seem to be having the time of our lives.

# Chapter 11

As predicted I did struggle with this training program, but I would finally successfully complete it. I was now living in the Orange County area, a friend of mine from work and I moved in together and we both had young sons, so we decided we needed four bedrooms and a large kitchen.

We were happy and drinking alcohol was now an everyday event for both of us.

I am going to take you back to my past a little further, so I can tell the next part of this story without confusing you and or myself. My mother came to visit us during Christmas for a couple of weeks and we all took turns on cooking dinners.

My female cousin called my mother one day while I was at work. She asked if she could come to visit us. My mother told her to come from her home which was located in Sacramento. She told my cousin she could stay with us for a couple of days. I was told about this that night when I had arrived at home and agreed with my mom it was okay, we had plenty of room. When the doorbell rang that night, I went to the door to welcome my cousin to my home.

I opened the door and saw cousin and went to give her a hug and then I saw HER. It was the one woman I had come to dislike with a passion that was very fierce and unfriendly. She was the very same woman I had met at my cousin's party some years back.

I informed my cousin that everyone was in the kitchen and she went in to say hello. As this tall Latina stepped up to my door, I looked at her and then told her that I was taught to be a gracious host. She was welcome to enter my house, but her opinions would not needed or required while she was staying with us.

As she started to enter my home, I simply stated that three males resided in this dwelling and everyone else was a guest. She walked by me and as she brushed my shoulder with hers she looked me in the eyes and said "We will see about that". As the visitation was in the second hour, my roommate and I decided to take the ladies to a club that was playing music. I told my roommate to keep the tall Latina busy, while I spent time with my cousin to see what her problems were at her home.

I then asked my cousin to dance and she said, "OK." We were on the dance floor and before I knew what I had happened her tall friend had joined us. The night ended as quickly as it had started and we all said good-night. The next night we decided to take the ladies to our favorite Country Western bar where we were well known. As we were drinking and playing our favorite music in the Jukebox. This newly found woman informed me my mother had told her I could two step dance.

I told her that my mother had told her the truth about my dancing ability. She than asked me, if I would teach her to two step? I answered yes I would teach her and proceeded to the Jukebox and put some of my favorite two stepping music on.

I then stepped onto the dance floor and told her I was ready. She then told me she did not want to learn in front of everyone. I asked the bartender to turn the music on outside, so we went outside and we began to dance. I noticed right off the lady had rhythm. Within a couple of songs she had become quite good at following my steps.

The next surprise was about to hit me full force. My roommate, my best friend had put on my favorite slow song and I told her the dance lesson was over. She asked me if I knew a step to this song and I answered yes. So we began to dance and somewhere during this song, the dancing ended and the kissing began. After several minutes we decided to walk back into the bar. As we walked in we couldn't help but notice eyes were upon us.

My friend was smiling and my cousin was shaking her head. I told my group of four people, it was time for us to go home, so we finished our drinks and went back to my safe haven.

Everyone went to bed and I went to the kitchen and finished cleaning it up for the next day's activities. As I was cleaning I noticed this lady I once hated was standing and watching me clean. I asked her if there was a problem with her bedroom and she replied no. She went on to enlighten me with her intent. She wanted to know what I thought about the evening's events and I responded with this gem of an answer. I was not ready for a long distant relationship and really didn't think I would be ready any time soon.

She was now standing against my kitchen pantry doors and wanted to know what the kissing was all about? I threw my sponge down and I walked over to her and with my hands I pressed her against the doors and informed her, how much I hated her and how close she had come to me and physical abuse. She than asked me if I really wanted to abuse her or would I rather do something else? I stepped closer to her and started to kiss her once again. We finally said good-night and went to our assigned bedrooms. Needless to say I did not sleep well that night and was one of the first into the kitchen to start cooking breakfast.

Everyone began to filter down stairs and pitched in on the preparation of the food. The girls told us they would be leaving after breakfast, so as a good host I volunteered to take the car and fill it up with gas and have it washed. I asked for the keys and my new friend asked if she could come along and I told her that would be okay. As they were washing her car we walked over the grassy area and began to talk about what we were feeling. I told her that the following week-end my friend was taking my son to his friend's house and they intended to return the day after New Year's.

Then I asked her if she wanted to come back and spend the week-end with me? She answered no thank-you; she did not know me well enough. I said I respected her decision and we went back to my home.

As the girls prepared to leave and we said our good-byes.

Additionally the next day my mother went home and I started to get ready to go to work. I had decided to make one phone call. It was to the Airlines that operated at my new friend's airport in the town she resided in and made a reservation for her on the Friday that was coming and returning on the Sunday. Anyone with basic logic would have asked me what I intended to do if she never called.

This relationship had nothing to do with logic and on Wednesday, the lady called and asked if I was serious with my invitation? I answered; I was so serious that I had already made a reservation for her. As I would find out as this relationship grew, this would be a relationship of who was in charge.

What A surprise that I would be on the submissive side of this relationship. I would lose many battles over the next twelve years. There would be a lot of great times, but the times which turned out to be disastrous, these situations would either temporarily end the relationship or end up in a shouting match that I would continue to lose.

Now before I continue with this portion of my story, I would like for you to understand how I am today versus my past. I was making decisions with a mind that had been saturated with alcohol and drugs. After all I was lacking confidence as a young man and I choose to defeat that weakness with a massive amount of alcohol. The effort I was trying so hard to accomplish in proving I was deserving of the job title would drain me and the only way to keep up the façade was to mask it with alcohol.

When a person gets to this point in life, it because easier to allow fantasy to replace reality.

I wanted to believe a woman could love me and I was willing to endure verbal and sometimes physical abuse.

Now that my mind is clear, I now know why running away was my answer to all my problems. To some this may sound as a cop out or a lame excuse as to why I was never successful when it came to emotional relationships. I would like to think today I am better equipped and becoming a stronger mentally. Now I will continue with this story in hopes that I am on a better road to recovery.

As I was saying earlier in this chapter, the relationship I found myself in seemingly the bad times would overrule over any good times we would share.

So many times we talked about marriage and spending the rest of our lives together. The day finally came to make our commitments to each other and marriage. It was at this time, I was informed that our plans had changed somewhat and I could not wait to hear these new changes.

The first change that had to be made was I was not going to be able to utilize my motor home.

This was followed by the announcement that my indented brides daughter was tired of caring for her three children that she had brought into this world. They were all going to move in with us.

This included the three children, her daughter and any boyfriend she choose.

The next changed was a complete surprise to me. I was going to be assigned the household duties of cooking all the meals.

Since my bride to be worked from 8:00am tile 5:00pm Monday through Friday. Additionally I was going to be responsible for the children to accomplish their chores, homework and any other duty they might be assigned. To say that I refused her proposal is stating lightly. I made it very clear not only was I not going to do what was being asked of me, rather I decided to put end to the relationship.

This came as a complete surprise to my ex-girlfriend. As tears formed in eyes she would ask me on more questions.

How could I say that I was in love with her if I was unwilling to do these things that were being asked of me? I countered with, what did our love have to do with changing our lives completely? Because her daughter was no longer willing to fulfill her obligations to her children?

As I packed my belongings, I started to think about all that had happen. Was I really that bad of a person or was my refusal of her request the smart move to make? I loaded up my luggage with my possessions and as I turned to leave, I gave my key back to my ex-girlfriend.

Without saying another word I left. I best sum up my relationship with this woman in the following manner.

We spent a good portion of our time, either intoxicated, high or a combination of both. The majority of the rest of the time, was spent yelling and screaming at each other.

The $50,000.00 question was why would two people stay together for so long? In my case, it was a matter entertainment and nothing better to do. At the end of the relationship, she was looking for a way to bring extreme pain into my life and possibly wanted to kill me and I was looking for a way out. We were two people who could not build a life together.

I may have been and a party animal or power drinker, but I knew this relationship was not going to work. We would talk about these things later, as we tried to remain friends.

She only came to see me once while I was sick two years after our break-up and she only had two or three hours' time to spend I would retire from the FAA in August of 2003. This retirement would last 5 months, I then decided to go back to work for a corporation who was contracted by the Federal Government. I was now a teacher of the job I had worked at for twenty six years. I was working in the same building I had left 5 months back. I was teaching the new ATC arrivals that were assigned to our area.

The lessons began with the basic airspace boundaries and ended with the sector that each new student would begin their training in.

My son I had decided to join the agency and become and follow in my footsteps. He went to college in Southern California. It was the only college certified by the FAA as a college that would assist in getting their students hire by the FAA. I would help by taking him and other students that were attending this college to different airports, so they could see firsthand what responsibilities were required to do the job.

# Chapter 12

I have left out the stories on my mistreatment of others, because they are a small fraction of pain I caused to all that I loved. My mother and father, my son, my sisters and brothers, and the rest of my close friends. I have not only been inconsiderate, but to say that I am somewhat cruel is putting my story in an honest text so people who have chosen to read this book will have a better understanding of who I truly am or who I was trying to be with my past activities. My failed love relationships and even some of my friendships have been an utter disappointment to me on all levels.

I blamed all of these and other problems I encountered on GOD. He was supposed to watch over me and give me guidance. The one problem I had was that I only talked to GOD when I needed him rather than every day. I never understood why he let these things happen to me. This would come to light later on when I was dying. GOD there for me, but I really never did stop to hear his message. Meanwhile I continued to blame GOD for my unhappiness and this would carry over when I first started on the path that would lead me to the five hospitals I would come in contact with, as the months would go by. To seek out who was at fault for my health and personal Problems all I had to do was look into the mirror. My life had quickly fallen apart and I was on the way off this earth for an eternal life hopefully with HE, I had come to know as my HIGHER POWER.

There were no more miracles or blessings available to me or at least that is what I thought at these desperate times and a life that seemed to be in complete shambles.

When I started to concede the fact that I and I alone was to blame for all that had happen to me. How was I going to correct these mishaps and was there going to be enough time for all that had to be done?

As you may remembered, what had occur to me when I was waking from my third coma, I felt GOD would not have sent me such a message if there was not going to be time for me to reach a conclusion. Where to start? Who would be first in line to hear my attempt at a sincere apology?

Why not try it on the one who was responsible for allowing me this extra time and was helping me restore my life and sanity.

All I had to be I thought, was be careful to watch for lightning bolts. When I saw the coast was clear, as far as nothing appearing from the sky, I started to put together my list of all those who had been effected by my actions and sometimes misuse of the English language. It was at this time I knew who was going to be the toughest one to talk to. My ex-wife and I had not spoken to each other for some twenty four years. The next one would have to be the woman I had a twelve year relationship with.

We had been broken up for almost three years at the time.

These two women would have to be dealt with first and with the up most sincerity. My family would not have to be told, what I had to do with them was show them through my actions that I was a changed person. I was going to get healthy enough to show them how I truly felt about them being there with me when the world came crashing down around me. I was going to make a commitment to say yes to their requests for my assistance on any level. Even if it would interfere with watching my favorite programs or sports teams which were being shown on TV.

# Chapter 13

My studies, of the working of AA were starting to take hold and I was beginning to understand that I was indeed not unique at all that I had destroyed. I no longer felt sorry for myself and was willing to do whatever it took to make things right with me and this world. The fact for some twenty six years I helped in defending our country had nothing to do with the pain and hurt I brought some unsuspecting people whose only fault was being in the same place as I happened to be at those auspicious times. To try to justify your good intentions with your bad ones was not a good solution for the pain I had caused.

When you are the one not living in reality, this point has a tendency to be covered up or even lost. You add the fact that you are still drinking and not ready to change or admit to your wrong doing may never will be brought to life.

You must be ready to do much more, change your whole life from your basic concept on what is wrong or right to how to solve the world's problems would be a start. What AA has taught me, is the world's problems are not mine to solve, since I cannot control any part of these problems. In addition I have learned to stay out of other people's business and to keep my opinions to myself.

The road ahead is still a long winding one, but one day at time has shown me to live in today. The weight of the world has been lifted and all that I carry with me is to remind myself to thank GOD for allowing me another day of life.

So with this working for me, my Love life was still in shambles.

I have certainly waited for a long time to try and meet the one woman who was right for me. My past, is best left alone in the past, since going back in time is an option not available to me. I continue to learn from my past experiences, because I do not want to repeat my mistakes again in case the one woman should enter my life.

My last tragedy in a love experience is somewhat on my mind and still had left my heart in disarray. The one affected by all this, is of course yours truly, because letting go of the past had never been easy for me to do. I have a new found commitment to continue my pursuit I improving in all areas, but so far the progress had seemed to be rather slow and had caused more problems than solving them. I do want to become a better person in all facets of life, more importantly the effects I have on others' lives.

The one marriage I was involved with had still left me wondering if I am suitable to be a partner for this precious woman and relationship.

Was she going to be a woman who had been through enough pain and hurt in her experience with those she choose to be her mate. I find myself asking more questions than there are answers for. So what is the right direction to pursue happiness with the one woman whom in my thoughts was meant for me and me alone? You would think at the tender age of fifty seven that this would have been answered by now. My family and I seemingly have reconciled on all levels and are now much happier than we have ever been. Those who still call me a friend have come to know a new me in a lot of new areas.

Strangers seemingly smile and shake my hand when we Are introduced. It would appear in some cases I am making positive movement forward. This road still has a lot of travels and adventures on it.

My health is improving day to day and I continue to monitor my vitals very closely. Taking my medications is no longer an issue and I am very aware of the consumption of drinks and food. Exercising this tired aging body has become my way to help release the stress life brings upon me. Sometimes living in reality has its bad moments. The only real conclusion I can draw is life by yourself, with no one to hold you and give the feeling of importance is missing and brings an empty sadness.

Is there any blessings left for me or have I used all of those up as well? They say time heals all wounds, well all I know is time maybe running out for me. Living on borrowed time has a way of making even the simplest of decisions somewhat difficult and stressful. This maybe my punishment for all of the damages I have caused and responsible for. Sometimes I feel I am caught between what I use to be like and what I believe myself to be like today. Is there someone out there who I have yet made amends to? I have searched for these answers relentlessly and I am no closer to the answers than I was three years ago, when my health went to hell and almost took my life with it. I do know this, I am so lucky to find the one, who can understand what I have endured through my own stupidity? Even worst, will she decide the best thing to do is pass me by because of the effort she will have to subject herself to help me understand the right from wrongs of those problem areas I still have not mastered?

# Chapter 14

Well we have come to the part of this book to leave you to draw your own conclusions as to what awaits me in my future. My final opinions or assumptions will be left to you and what you may think I deserve or what will be my punishment. I would like you to know this little tad bit, whatever awaits me I have no one to blame but myself and I am willing to bear the full brunt of all my mistakes and errors in judgment. Before you decide on my fate, please keep in mind that in trying to change my life around to take full advantage of my second chance, I am still the stubborn, sometimes frustrated man I have always been.

I also know I am still capable of repeating some of my many mistakes again.

I would start to wonder if he, my Higher Power thought I was deserving of any further blessings or if you prefer the word, miracles. This would be something I would see unfold before me soon. I had learned to talk to my Higher Power with the utmost respect.

Questions kept mounting but for the most part they would be answered as soon as GOD thought I had earned them, I was willing to know the true answers. In the year of 2010, I found out I had not used all of my blessings, miracles or whatever you chose to call them up. My Higher Power, He who I call GOD has given me three treasures that cannot be replaced or even explained, so that logic may be evoked to explain how these three small blessing have found their way into my life. The first blessing that was bestowed upon me came to me via my doctor. As soon as I were told I was in need of a liver transplant my son stepped forward and volunteered to give me a piece of his liver. This would have to be accomplished by way of he becoming my live donor. We filed the paper work that would be needed to get him transferred from the LA area to Northern California. Once this was completed and approved by the Federal Government, he and his new family moved to my part of the world. He started along with doctors here to run the needed test for him to prove he was healthy enough to become my donor.

This took about a year and he passed the entire test required. When it came to the last test and he went my Liver Hospital for the final test. He would not fare well on this test. The results came back and said my son had a blood clotting problem. This would eliminate him from the program, unless he would be willing to seek out his own doctor and correct the problem. He really wanted to be my donor, so he would accomplish this task. The next blessing came to me in February of the same year. My son and daughter-n-law presented me with my first and only blood related Grand Daughter.

To say she looks Latina would be somewhat of a falsehood. She arrived with red Hair, pale skin and blue eyes. Along with this precious gift three more children came to me from my daughters prior marriage. These three blessings learned to call me Grand Pa and I like the way that sounds every time I visit them. Instead of one I now have four wonderful Grand Children who I have a great deal of Love for. The third of these small blessings came to me in July, my Doctors said my health was making such a big turnaround, they agreed that early next year I will be taken off the active Liver Transplant list and moved to the Inactive one.

This means of course my health along with my Liver were responding to my commitments and daily activities and as long as I did not encounter any other problems with my Liver. The doctors informed me I could live for a good many years, that is as long as I do not pick up another drink that contained alcohol in it. As stated earlier why would I want to extend my life without the one person who is truly missing? To answer this question I would like to take you back to the moment I was awakening from my third Liver induced Coma for one more visit. The voices said my work had not been accomplished here on earth.

What does this have to with finding the right woman for me? Let me take you back even further into my past.

When I was a very young seventeen year old teenager as I eluded earlier in this book, I met that young and so innocent Hispanic Sixteen year old who had fallen in, what can be best described as puppy love with me at a time I felt I did not deserve such feelings. I had left her behind and not even given her another thought. The thing I want you to remember, I left this young lady behind without any word or explanation of my actions. How could I know the damage that I had caused by my actions so early in my life, but damage was indeed done and once again I have no one to blame but myself. As stated earlier I would go on to marry in 1975 to another young lady I had become quite fond of in the last year of High School. The marriage would last ten years and she did manage to give me a son. The divorce was a rather painful and bitter one and I ended up losing everything I had worked so hard for. This would leave such a bitter taste in my mouth; I would swear to never marry again. Meanwhile as to what happen to the young lady I left behind, she also would get married and give birth to two children, one boy and one girl.

But what of that young lady I left behind?

**HAD SHE ONCE EVER THOUGHT OF ME AND WHAT HAD BECOME OF HER LIFE?**

# Chapter 15

Now we fast forward to March of 2010 . . . It had been one year since my last operation that would repair my damaged hernia. I was asleep one evening and was about to have a dream that would throw me for a loop.

Before enlightening about the dream, let me reflect back on my awakening from the third coma I suffered, those voices I had heard were described to me as a hallucination. My work had not yet been completed here on earth. Naturally I thought these words were directed for me to help those who were lost like I was and they needed to know their future and how to change their lives around.

Were they going to accomplish this by themselves? Was it going to be easy or was going to take work?

Well back to the dream I was now about to come face to face with. I was at this formal engagement and I was standing alone sampling some of the foods and beverages served. As I was standing and eating, a woman walked by me and I happened to notice she was, what I would described as a pretty Latin woman about my age. I did not recognize her, but in trail of her was another woman who called to her as they were passing me and she used her first name, a name I had not heard in almost forty years.

It so happened to be the name of the young woman I had left behind when I was seventeen. I laid my plate down and turned to follow the two women, they had exited the room and by the time I saw her again she was climbing a spiral staircase. Half way up she stumbled and lost her balance and came back down in a rather dangerous fashion. I ran to the bottom of the staircase in time to grab her as she was about to hit the floor. I looked at her face and still could not put the looks with the name. As I looked at her face, I looked into her eyes and to my surprise did not see pain, but rather years of sadness and what thought was a broken heart.

This pretty lady then reached out her arms, with tears in her eyes she called out my name. This was unexpected and I did not know if she would hear me if I spoke to her. I thought to myself, who was responsible for the hurt this woman was expressing and what had she done to deserve such treatment? The dream ended and I awoke and could not make heads or tails of the meaning of the dream. So I decided the best thing to do was to forget the dream and not say anything about it to anyone.

About a week later I would have the same dream again and once again it ended as it had before.

That very night, the next dream, number two, enter my sleep. This dream showed me the same woman and she was married and had two children.

The first part of this dream showed her to be happy, and then once again the sadness returned. This time it seemed to me someone she knew had ripped her heart apart. The second dream ended and this time I was sure these dreams were pointing me in a direction. Was this the same person and was I the one that had hurt this pretty lady? The next morning I awoke and told my mother about the two dreams and then asked her for an opinion. She thought possibly the dreams were telling me to go and find this woman. I countered with, what if I did find her? What was I supposed to tell her or even ask her and how much was I supposed to tell her about what had happened to me?

Other questions started to become clear, what if she was still married or even worse, what if she could not remember who I was? Then the most obvious question hit me full force. How was I going to find her? I did not know what last name she was using, since by now she must have married. Then the next questioned followed.

What state in the USA was I going to start my search for her in? I decided the best thing to do was to sit and ponder the dreams and try to solve them myself.

This would be a rather futile event and most certainly a waste of my time and effort. Since I owned my own computer, I decided to seek out some of her friends we both knew when we were young. I came across a couple of friends and started to correspond with them. I asked them of either one of them knew what had happen to the young lady I knew as my first Love? They knew some information, but knew nothing of her where about at this current time.

Frustration would soon set in and I grew tired of coming up empty every direction I choose to follow. The search would end and I felt certain I was not going to be able to locate her.

I couldn't help but wonder if forty years was too much time to let pass. The dreams had come to a complete stop and I was finally at peace once again. A month or two passed and my health was improving rather nicely and I was at my son's home playing with my Grand Daughter, this was becoming really enjoyable since she now was starting to recognize me.

My AA program was coming along nicely and I was starting to voyage into the prison systems to hold meetings for the inmates that were searching for answer of their own. What of the lady I was searching for?

If I found her, would she be able to enlighten me further on occurrences my dreams had shown me? What had happened to this young lady with her marriage and children? What city she was possibly living in? The dreams returned and the rotation of the two stayed the same. Luck found a way to find me. I noticed one day on the computer link I had visited before, there was a spot that listed friends these two ladies I had written before and happened to notice a woman that had the same last name as the lady I was in search of. Without hesitating I clicked on their friend and it turned out to be her older sister.

I had never met this person before, so writing her seems to be a lousy way of introducing myself and trying to find the location of her sister. This woman had some photo albums of her and her family, so I decided to look to see if I could find my Lady of the past. To my surprise I found a picture of her mom, her and the young lady I had left behind. The two other women were smiling, but my lady (the woman who was in my dreams) I had left behind, had a look of seriousness about her. I printed a copy and showed the picture to my mom. She agreed that my lady did not look happy.

What I did not know was that my mother and younger sister were becoming somewhat frustrated with me and my pursuit of this person. They both came to me one day and volunteered to take me to the last known location of the woman I was seeking and after a couple of minutes I decided against this suggestion and sort of promised I would never bring her up again.

Once again the dreams stopped for a time, but they return a month later. This time a third dream was including in the package of the two prior dreams. This dream indicated we had met and were happy with each other, a relationship broke out and we decided to move in together.

Everything was going along nicely and we decided that marriage together was our next step. As we were planning the event one evening and then she received a phone call from one of her relatives asking her to help with a situation. In this dream, I did all that I could to assure my wife to be that I supported her decision as to flying to see her family to assist with her support. I made the arrangements for the flight and our arrival to the airport. As we were in line to go through security at the airport, A thought entered my mind and it simply indicated that this would be the last time I would see this woman I had searched for such a long time. I went home and started to prepare myself for the future. At first the phone calls between us came in rather regular intervals. As time went on the phone calls started to come less and less.

These calls would soon come to end and my nightmares started. How was I going to live without her? Where would my happiness come from? The dream ended with me living alone and I made new commitments to my AA Program. With my health still on the improvement side, I started to search for the lady who had entered my dreams and was starting to become more that just a concern me. My mother and sister were getting more frustrated with me once again as I kept bringing her up in our conversations. I went to visit a lady who seemed to know the most about the woman who had taken over my dream world. She informed me she now knew where the was living. When I got home I once again went to my computer and I decided to write her sister on my favorite computer link explaining briefly who I was and I was seeking for her younger sister. I informed her. I had been given some information about the town her sister was living in and I was hoping that she would respond to my request. The next day I opened my computer and there was a response from the elder sister. She had talked to her sister and her sister had indicated she did not know me.

She went on to tell me that the two of them were concerned, that I possessed knowledge of where she was living. As I read this first response to my E-Mail, something happened to me I was not quite prepared for. Even though I knew there was a possibility this pretty lady would not remember me, I would have preferred to hear that she was married or involved with another man than to the truth.

As the truth began to unfold itself before me, the fact was the lady did not remember me, but was rather concerned how I knew about her residence. As the tears began to roll off my cheeks, I remembered looking up at the ceiling and asking GOD if this was his dea of letting me know the punishment and sadness He felt I was due?

What was I supposed to learn from this lesson? I already knew I was guilty of bad decisions and the terrible and at times the brutal behavior I had administered to all those innocent people that had come across my life.

I then began to recall the loneliness I felt when the doctors had told me to go home and die, some months before. But this, this was a depth of loneliness that certainly bring to my knees and pray for a quick end to the pain that engulfed me. All I could do was sit there and shake my head as I looked up. I was done thinking of anymore alternatives, all I wanted was to lie down and wait for my Higher Power to come and get me. Certainly I would fare better in my new eternal home than I had in the one I had come to know for so many years. The next thought that hit me, were both of these ladies thinking I was pursuer of women or even worst, was I a pervert of some sort. Once again I looked at the heavens above and asked GOD if this is what he intended for me? I then asked for his guidance to assist me with my next move. I sat there for quite a while and then the answer came to me.

I decided to take another chance and write her sister again, this time explaining how her sister and I met and what we had shared. I concluded this message with, if her sister did not remember me. I would no longer peruse any further communication with either one of them. Once again the next day I opened up my computer and there was a response to my note form her sister. I was sort of afraid to open it up, what if her sister thought I was a stalker or other perverted type of individual?

As scared as I was I opened up the note and she informed me that her sister knew who I was, with the new information given her and she told her sister to give me her cell phone number because she wanted to talk to me.

So on the first Sunday in September of 2010 I called this woman. Now normally I would not have made this phone call, after all it was the first Sunday of football season.

Since my team was in the mist of being beaten and it was half time. I made the call, I could only imagine that this phone call would last for five minutes or less.

This would be time enough for me to reintroduce myself and to enlighten her briefly as to what had prompted this call. I had long waited to find this woman and asked if the dreams I was having made any sense to her? As I was rehearsing what I was going to say, she answered the phone, she answered before I was ready to proceed.

When she said hello, there was complete silence on the other end. She restated and said hello again and this time I responded, this would be the start of a three hour conversation between her and I.

I remember starting the conversation after our introductions that I was not a religious man, but what had happened to me after getting ill and suffering the three coma episodes. How I had made it through two operations I was not supposed to survive and what had happened while waking from my third coma. I went on to tell her, I was not asking, anything from her except possibly a clarification on the dreams and their meaning. We talked about everything we had been through and found ourselves laughing at a good portion of these tales. As the conversation was coming to a conclusion, I had finally notice the phone call had lasted three hours. I once again took a bold chance, a chance that I could not ever imagine me taking, I asked her if she would join me for a dinner date. As I waited her answer, I realized I had opened the conversation by stating I would not ask for a thing from her. To my surprised she answered yes and we set the date for the following Saturday. As we said our good-byes I could tell something had happened between us that I was not expecting. Then another surprised happen to me. My ex-girlfriend called me and told me why she could not answer my phone call. She wanted to send me an E-Mail instead. I then informed her I had found the woman I had been searching for.

We had set up a date and I was looking forward to seeing her again. The next day my ex-girlfriend sent me the E-Mail.

In this letter was information that was basic in understanding. She informed me I was guilty of ripping her heart out and she was sorry she had dated me. In conclusion I was informed that if I was not satin himself, I was a close relative his. The next day I called my new friend and again and we spent three hours talking and laughing in recanting some more of our adventures we had survived. She had been married before and had given birth to two children, one boy and a girl.

I had shared some of my relationships including my marriage and explained the disastrous conclusions. I could sense the inability for us both to say good-bye and conclude the conversation. I then informed her I would not call her again, so that I would not become a pest of any sorts to her. She responded with, and then I guess I will call you tomorrow. The next day she called and once again the call lasted almost three hours and this time she concluded the call with she wanted to see me before Saturday. We made arrangement to meet at her job on Thursday of that week and give ourselves the opportunity to see one another. To my surprise we decided to not share any further communications on Wednesday.

I went to her job on Thursday and as I walked in and spotted her, I had noticed she had not seen me enter, so I walked over to the next aisle and began to watch her as she was having a conversation with a customer. I was enjoying myself observing her, you see I had not expected her to be so young and pretty, besides her pretty features, she had an energy level of a much younger woman. She was nothing like me, rather worn and old. The customer left and she turned around and notice I was looking at her. She asked me if I was the man she was waiting for and I shook my head no.

She continued to look at me and then I finally could not hold back any further, and answered yes. She came over and gave me a hug. We spent a moment reintroducing ourselves to each other and I found myself staring into her eyes as to be looking for answers. I had bought her a small gift and she accepted it and we started to talk about what we we're expecting from this first meeting. She then informed me her shift had ended and it was time for her to leave. I suggested, since we had a date coming up on Saturday, would it be alright if I followed her home to see where she resided? She answered with yes that would be alright, so we left. We got to her home and she invited me inside and we sat and talked for four or five hours and as I was leaving her once again stood in front of me with that same pretty smile she possesses. I walked up to her as she repeated the identical kiss she had given me when we were young. As I kissed her good bye this time I sensed this was not going to be the only time we would share a moment like this. Saturday came and as I was getting prepared for our first date, I started to get nervous. Here I am, an aging old man and I had survived three comas and an illness that was supposed to take my life and I am getting nervous about meeting a woman I knew forty years ago?

Anyway I arrived at her home at the prescribe time and we went to dinner at one of her favorite restaurants. We were seated and a conversation broke out as if we had never been apart. Dinner went well and we returned to her home and once again we sat apart, her on her sofa and I was seated on her love seat. We talked for quite a while and then I prepared myself to depart and I looked at her and asked, was this end of our meetings or did she want to continue with this relationship? She answered yes, that she wanted to continue.

So I asked her when she would like to go out again.

She informed me that Friday or Saturday worked best for her. I responded with any day was good for me, after all I was retired. That was not what I really wanted to say to her.

After all I had searched for this woman for almost a year. I Had certainly been through a lot recently and who knew if I had another tomorrow left to me. There were so many topics I would have loved to have attempted to discuss with her, including why I never came back to at least talk to her.

# Chapter 16

We went on a dates a couple of more times to and we were getting closer as far having real feelings for each other. One night after we returned from dinner we were talking about the times we had spent together when we were younger and then the subject turned to the letter she had sent me when we were teenagers that I never responded to. She looked at me and began to enlighten me how she felt when I had left without ever saying another word to her, either by mail or orally. What I observed was her expression which had changed from the smile I was getting to know and the sadness that was as apparent as she continued with her feelings at the time.

This would be the first time I would notice, she had the same look on her face now that she had in my dreams.

She finished with her story, it would have been nice if I had at least sent her some kind of explanation instead of my silence. I stood up and said good night and kissed her and left to go to my home. By the time I had reached home, I knew I needed to write her a letter and try to explain what all went through my mind the last night we spent together when we were young. When I got home I turned on my computer and started to type a letter addressed to her entitled "Forty Years Later". If I had only one wish to give to you, that wish would be that you find a way in your heart to forgive me. I did not do or say that which was truly in my heart forty years ago. I had a heart that belonged to a young, scared man. My feelings in my heart were taken over by the thoughts of my own weaknesses and inadequacies. I am guilty of leaving a young beautiful woman, a woman I was in LOVE with, but thought I was not worthy of her LOVE. I did this with complete silence and without explanation. Little did I know the hurt and confusion that this young teenage woman would have to carry with her, with no answer to her haunting question? WHY? I only have these words to offer this woman today.

I promise I will do my best to prove to you, while proving to myself, that I will never again be afraid to say that which is in my heart. Additionally I promise I will do all I can to make sure from now on, the only tears you will know, will be tears of happiness.

I am flawed and like all men in this world, I will make a mistake from time to time. I will never again run away from the truth and reality. If I am fortunate to receive your forgiveness, then please let the past go. I know this is easy for me to request, but it must be very difficult for you to accept. I made a mistake and I wish to apologize for my lack of consideration of your feelings or hard it must have been for you to accept what I must have put you through. I choose to run away and I thought I was giving you the opportunity to find yourself a better young man who could give you all that you deserved. I was wrong and I am truly sorry for this incident.

Finally, I now know why GOD made finding you so important. I needed to not only see and hear all the damage I have caused, but the forgiveness you possess. I know that I am forty years late in getting this message to you. Once again I ask for your continued love and friendship.

A LONG LOST FRIEND,

In this letter was meant to explain all that had gone through my mind after leaving her home and why I kept my silence even after she sent her letter. I would go on to tell her how wrong I now knew I was in doing this, she did deserve an explanation and I could not bring myself to accomplish this. I apologized for my behavior and was hoping to be forgiven for my lack of action.

She read the letter the next time we were together and she turned to me and smiled. She informed me that she would forgive me as long as my running away from her was over and to discontinue to remind her of our past.

At least now I knew more about dream number one. I was partially to blame for the sadness in her eyes and I had never even given this matter a thought. As for what had happened in dream number three, she said she did not know what this meant. She had relatives living in another state but had not really kept up with them. She did have her son who was living in another state and he was married. As far leaving me behind she did not know what to make of that either. Needless to say the relationship started to bloom into a LOVE relationship and we were both in favor of what was happening between us. We started to see more of each other and finally as my family was convinced we had become inseparable. Time had come for us to meet each other's families and all went well for us and we started to see a road that was ours to travel together. In meeting her family I was introduced to her son and daughter and their significant partners at a family event.

Everyone was very cordial and the atmosphere was very relaxed and full of laughter. The week-end before, I had introduced her to my family. My parents and she hit off immediately. They were very relaxed with each other and conversation seemed to come with no reservations.

As you may well know all relationships go through their growing pains and our is no different. We started to see them come to light as we spent more and more time together. We have shared our feelings on possibly moving in together and even had a conversation on getting married. The future is ours to have and enjoy, we also know that when we are apart from each other we are not as happy as we are when we spend quality time together.

We both know what we have survived disheartening and abusive relationships. What we knew the type of relationship we would no longer tolerate from our partners as far as conduct and how important true communication is.

What then is left for me to tell you about the direction my life might be headed for, or where my decisions good or bad might help me with my future. You can draw your own conclusions as far as where my newly found LOVE and I are headed. Will this truly be the last time I have to make a stand by myself and has GOD brought us together for the rest of our lives? What is truly left of existence? I now feel more than ever with these three new blessings, life is good and I want and desire to live for as long as my Higher Power allows me to stay here and continue to improve in all facets of life.

I decided it was time for me to apologize for my actions and thoughts I was guilty of before our first date. I knew she was not aware of, since they were of a not so respectable thought. I had packed an overnight bag while I was getting ready for our first date. I know, how could I be so bold as to think she was going to ask me to spend the first night together? We both laughed and she couldn't stop herself from asking me the one question that had come to her mind. What would I have done if she had asked me to spend the night with her? I did not know the answer to the question, but I like to think that I am a true gentleman.

Well since then, we have decided to move in together and started to make arrangements for our upcoming marriage.

We want our children to be involved and we have decided to keep this event only to our family and close friends. We plan to move back to the small town I grew up in and we await her job to transfer her. We now believe we belong together for the rest of our lives and we are both committed to this belief. She has stated, she let me get away from her one time that will not occur this time.

Our families thoroughly believe we belong together. We seem to keep them laughing and we are never far away from each other.

In fact if we are not holding hands we are sitting next to each other or she is seated on my lap.

As for me I am truly happy and the thoughts of ever picking up another alcohol drink have dwindled. My love for our families and for the woman continues to grow. I continue to educate myself in all aspects of life and only wish to prosper in whatever GOD deems the best for me.

Time will tell what road I will choose to follow and I can only hope I stay on the path that lays in front of me now.

Surprises still seem to throw me at times. This particular one did, finding my true love.

The day came for us to join hands and to vow our love to each other and the ceremony went as plan. I was showing no signs of nervousness and I believed that I was going to complete our vows without a hitch. I did well up until putting the ring on her finger. Since I had opted not to wear my glasses, a small flaw in my plan brought a bit of laughter out of the crowd. The rings had not been joined permanently and without my glasses I could not see them well enough to join them together prior to attempting to place them on her proper finger. My best man assisted me, but had to put in his two cents. The ceremony was all that we had planned for. We will have fond memories of the days event.

My life has been steadily improving since my earlier battles to stay alive. The marriage has had its moments, but both of us feel that we can stand together and face the battles yet to be fought. My new wife, while preparing for my upcoming doctors visit came up to me and informed me, if indeed I was going to need a liver transplant, she was willing to become my live donor. The look on my face must have said it all. One other thought I will share with you, true love has found its way into my heart and I want to stay committed to honesty, compassion and forgiveness. It is my personal belief that when you truly find the true LOVE meant to be by your side, you must do everything possible to ensure that eternity means forever. Find every answer and do not give up on the solutions to make this union the best for the two of you. When your heart is content and beats without pain or hesitation you will know you have succeeded. All these tools have been given to me through my relationship with AA and my Higher Power. Will my words be backed up by my actions or am I—.

My last thought for a conclusion is very simple. For the first time I know where to go, now that the party is over. The only question that remains is do I have what it takes to follow through with the commitments and obligations of sworn to uphold. These are Promises I have made to myself, my wife, family and GOD.

I know this book will be not to everyone's liking, but I wanted to share with all that took time to read this, I am a better person today than I was when I was drinking and using. I am only a person, like anyone else, with good and bad. Each of us deserves a fair and a equal opportunity to live the best life that we can. All I want is my past to be my past and for my present and future to be how I will be remembered. THANK-YOU!

THE END

# MY THOUGHTS ON HOW I VIEW DAILY LIFE

As you awake each morning and prepare yourself for the days adventures, you must remember you have been given the blessing of facing another day. My only wish is that you spend this day to learn how to become a better person than you were yesterday.

Washing and dressing yourself are only some of the simple tasks, you must also ensure you are properly equipped with all the necessities to aide you in facing life's trials and tribulations.

Your personal bag of tools maybe one these aides. These tools must consist of important and usable lessons and wisdom gained from past mistakes and they may also include achievements gained from goodness, fairness and just behavior.

As you start to walk on your road set out for you, it is Important to remember to watch each step you take. This act has been described as a person who is living in the present. Someone who is willing to whatever barriers or problems that life has a tendency to throw at you. Then when time presents itself, remember to take a quick glance at the road ahead. Planning your next step may assist you in staying away from yesterday's mistakes.

Understand this, life has no guarantees, but with your bag of tools of wisdom gained, do not forget to reach in when the situation calls, this will give you a better method to finding the best solution.

The road of reality continues because it is never ending.

Confusion, frustrations and at time situations that may cause anger seemingly surrounds you. Do not allow yourself to jump to conclusions or even worst, to utter words of destruction or violence. This behavior brings the same solution as those who choose to bang their bodies against that brick wall that has stood in front of us all at the most inopportune time.

You must know by now, you do not possess the tools that will bring that wall down. There is no shame in finding a way around that stack of bricks. Pride is the correct feeling, after all you have become a better person by learning from past mistakes. Store this knowledge in your bag, you may have need of this important information again. As you continue down your road, it is important to note your bag of tools continue to grow with each lesson learned. Do not lose focus on the present or your carefully thought out goals, this will continue to insist you in seeing possible holes or turns that your road has provided.

Then without even a thought of your achievements, someone may come up to you and offer his or her hand to you in friendship. This maybe one of your enlightening moments. This hand that has been extended to you could be a sign that someone has noticed your newly acquired smile and possibly the sincerity that you now possess in your eyes. Do not be surprised, your heart maybe beating in total agreement.

# DEDICATION

This book was written for all those unfortunates that suffer And sometimes died from the same disease that found its way into my life. Additionally, the finding of a Higher Power known to me as GOD has helped me to find a new peace in my heart.

To my family that showed me compassion and LOVE when death was so near?

To my Grand Children that have Blessed my life with their Presence. The truest of Blessings that GOD could have ever bestowed upon me.

The finding of a woman I left behind when we were so young. To know that true LOVE was there all along and I was to blind and immature to recognize that the one woman who could complete me has once again found a place Into my HEART.

A special thanks for my step son, nephew, and my own son, who have assisted me in writing these words and designing this presentation to you.